Growing for God

Simon J Robinson

Day One

© Day One Publications 2001
First printed 2001

Scripture quotations are taken from The New International Version.© 1973, 1978, 1984, International Bible Society. Published by Hodder and Stoughton.

British Library Cataloguing in Publication Data available
ISBN 1 903087 14

Published by Day One Publications
3 Epsom Business Park, Kiln Lane, Epsom, Surrey KT17 1JF.
01372 728 300 **FAX** 01372 722 400
email—sales@dayone.co.uk
www.dayone.co.uk

Designed by Steve Devane and printed by Redwood Books

To my wife Hazel

Contents

It has been salutary to read Simon Robinson's excellent little book on spiritual growth. His subject is of the moment for every Christian, since growth is an on-going process, in which there is no room for complacency. Spiritual growth can be lost so that there is need to begin all over again. God often has to show us what novices we are.

It has helpfully prompted reflection on some of the influences that have stimulated spiritual growth in my own life, all of which are reflected in the pages that follow. First was the encouragement to read, know, understand and apply the Scriptures to life. Soon after my conversion, I was recommended to look every day for some verse, phrase, or word from my Bible reading, to write it down, and then to think about it and turn over in my mind. The habit has now become almost second nature and I cannot measure how beneficial it has been.

Second, was the encouragement to pray with other Christians. Looking back, I recognise that spiritual growth was prompted, and desires for it increased, as I listened to older and more mature Christians pray. I longed to know God as they so evidently did. I learnt more from their prayers than they ever knew.

Third, was the benefit of unconscious role models of spiritual growth older Christians provided. I not only learnt much from their prayers but primarily through their character and behaviour. Without doubt, they were unconscious of their own growth, and the role model they provided, and I was unaware at the time of the significant influence they had upon me. However, I cannot think now of the example of their lives without thanking God for them and the stimulus they were, and remain, to my spiritual growth.

Fourth, was the influence of Christian books, and especially Christian biography. The first book I remember being given after my conversion was the story of Hudson Taylor. Later a birthday gift was his two-volume life, one of which is entitled 'The Growth of a Soul'—significant in view of the title of Simon Robinson's book. Lessons I learned from it have remained with me today. One passage, so relevant to me at the time and subsequently, I can recite from memory fifty years afterwards! 'How then to have our faith increased? Only by thinking of all that Jesus is, and all He is for us: His life, His death, His work, He Himself as revealed to us in the

Word, to be the subject of our constant thoughts. Not a striving to have faith, or to increase our faith, but a looking off to the Faithful One seems all we need; a resting in the Loved One entirely, for time and for eternity.'

Finally, as I have read Simon Robinson's book, I have recognised that perhaps the very best way of expressing spiritual growth is in terms of knowing God. John 17:3 is crucial to our understanding: 'Now this is eternal life: that they may know you, the only true God, and Jesus Christ, whom you have sent.' All true growth is growth in the knowledge of God, as we know His Son better. Put another way, spiritual growth is gaining more of Christ. It is not primarily a matter of method but of spiritual desire. As we recognise that apart from Him we have no good thing we are on the way to a right perspective for daily living and spiritual growth. John Pollock, D L Moody's biographer, found that the evangelist's most intriguing quality was his capacity for growth right until the end of his life. May this book contribute to that end in all of us who read it.

Derek Prime
Edinburgh

The growth gene

The excitement of Christmas Day had finally dissolved. Having caught up on lost sleep my sister and I tiptoed downstairs to play with our new toys. A few hours later we were eating our traditional Boxing Day dinner of cold turkey and baked potatoes, followed by warmed up Christmas Pudding. We had hardly finished our last mouthful when my mother broke the news; 'we are going to see your aunt this afternoon.' We looked at one another with shock. 'This afternoon?' we said with a mixture of outrage and disappointment, 'but it's Boxing Day and we've got all these toys to play with!' Having already prepared her counter attack, my mother gave us a knowing smile. 'I know it is,' she said understandingly, 'but your aunt wants to give you your presents.' That little piece of news changed everything; we could not wait to get there!

My aunt greeted us with her usual enthusiasm, 'How lovely to see you!' she said, 'and let me take a look at these children'. We knew exactly what was going to happen next. She would stand back, look us up and down, 'tut' a few times, draw us into a suffocating hug and, as she released us, she would tell us how much we had grown. 'I just cannot get over how much you've shot up since I last saw you,' she'd say. At the end of the visit we were herded back into the car, and in the short journey home my mind was spinning. 'Why did she say I've grown so much?' I thought. 'I do not seem to be any taller than when I looked in the mirror yesterday. And what's so surprising about it anyway?' Looking back, I realise she was just commenting on the fact that time had passed and nature had taken its course. If I had stayed the same size she would have been very worried.

You can probably remember something similar, but let us put it in a different setting. Imagine you meet up with a friend who had been a great help to you when you first became a Christian. Having not seen him for a long time you tell him about your job, your Church, your family, and catch up on his news. Would he be able to see signs of spiritual growth in your life, or would you be no different than when you last met? If you have not been growing as a Christian you should be very concerned, for, as physical growth is a normal part of our early years, spiritual growth is essential throughout our Christian life. And, unlike natural growth, it does not stop when we reach a particular age – it carries on until we get to heaven. Spiritual growth is not an optional part of the Christian life—it is a necessity.

The Peter Pan problem

When I was a child one of my favourite stories was 'Peter Pan.' It is about a boy who never grew up, which was an idea I found quite attractive! As time passed by I realised this was a complete fantasy; like it or not I had to accept new responsibilities and put childhood pleasures behind me. True as that may be, it does not always happen in the Church—in fact it is full of 'Peter Pans' – people who have never grown in their relationship with Christ. That is why I have written this book.

Tapping into the terminology

If we are going to think about spiritual growth it is important that we understand what it is.

There are three key words for growth in the New Testament. The first speaks of an increase in the blessing God has given to us, and in the work He is doing in our lives. In 1 Thessalonians Paul expresses a heartfelt desire that the Christians in Thessolonica 'increase and abound in love to one another' (1 Thessalonians 3:12). In his second letter he gives thanks that their faith is growing (2 Thessalonians 1:3).

The second word means 'to multiply' or 'to abound.' Luke uses it several times in Acts. It describes the new additions to the Early Church (Acts 6:1,7), and the way in which the Word of God spread across the region (Acts 12:24).

The third and most common word is about the process of growth. Jesus uses it to describe the way the lilies of the fields (Matthew 6:28), and trees grow (Mark 4:8). Luke makes use of it to tell us how John the Baptist and Jesus 'grew and became strong in spirit' (Luke 1:80, 2:40). The New Testament Letters, however, use this word to describe a process of spiritual growth, brought about by God. Paul reflects on the way in which this happened in the church at Corinth saying, 'I planted, Apollos watered, but God gave the increase. So then neither he who plants is anything, nor he who waters, but God who gives the increase' (1 Corinthians 3:6-7). Ephesians 2:21 pictures the Church as building which 'grows into a holy temple in the Lord.' And Ephesians 4:15 calls on us to 'speak the truth in love' so that we 'may grow up in all things into Him who is the head–Christ.'

This word is used on an individual level to call us to grow in faith (2 Corinthians 10:15), in the knowledge of God (Colossians 1:10), and in 'the grace and knowledge of our Lord and Saviour Jesus Christ' (2 Peter 3:18). Lawrence O. Richards says these two factors–natural and spiritual growth, to which this word refers, gives us great insight on the matter of spiritual growth: 'God has designed the individual and the church according to His perfect specifications. As we grow, we move toward a perfection that He has planned for us.'[1]

On the circumference or at the centre?

Sometimes I have heard people talking about spiritual growth as if it were one of the less important parts of the Christian life, but the New Testament gives us a very different picture. Growth is never suggested—it is commanded! We must 'leave the elementary teachings about Christ and go on to maturity, not laying again the foundation of repentance from acts that lead to death, and of faith in God', (Hebrews 6:1 NIV). And 'grow up in our salvation' (1 Peter 2:2).

It is also a goal we aim for. Paul said that He preached about Christ 'warning every man and teaching every man in all wisdom, that we may present every man perfect in Christ Jesus' (Colossians 1:28). 'Perfect' does not mean sinless but 'complete' or 'mature'. Epaphras, the Pastor of the Church in Colosse, fervently prayed that the people in his care 'may stand perfect and complete in all the will of God' (Colossians 4:12). And Paul spoke of his own determination to move forward.

'Not that I have already attained, or am already perfected; but I press on, that I may lay hold of that for which Christ Jesus has also laid hold of me. Brethren, I do not count myself to have apprehended; but one thing I do, forgetting those things which are behind and reaching forward to those things which are ahead, I press toward the goal for the prize of the upward call of God in Christ Jesus. Therefore let us, as many as are mature, have this mind; and if in anything you think otherwise, God will reveal even this to you. Nevertheless, to the degree that we have already attained, let us walk by the same rule, let us be of the same mind. (Philippians 3:12-16).

Lack of growth is dangerous because if we do not go forward—we'll slip back! Peter warns us not to 'fall from (our) secure position' but to 'grow in the grace and the knowledge of our Lord and Saviour Jesus Christ' (2 Peter 3:17-18 NIV). The choice is clear; we can either move forward or slide back. I grew up in a seaside town and spent a lot of time on boats. One day I had used up so much energy in rowing my boat I decided to take a rest. I laid my paddles down, stretched out my feet and closed my eyes. After a few minutes I opened them again, and I was horrified to find I had drifted quite a distance. In the end I had to use up twice as much energy to get my boat back to the shore. Similarly, we can never stay still in our Christian lives; we can go forward to greater maturity, or we can drift back. That is why spiritual growth is essential.

Lack of growth leads to spiritual immaturity, which creates chaos in churches. Take Corinth as an example. Paul laments that he cannot address them as 'spiritual people' but as those who were 'carnal' and 'babes in Christ' (1 Corinthians 3:1). This prevented them from being taught anything beyond the very basic doctrines: 'I fed you with milk and not with solid food; for until now you were not able to receive it, and even now you are still not able;' (1 Corinthians 3:2). And their immature behaviour divided the Church: 'for you are still carnal. For where there are envy, strife, and divisions among you, are you not carnal and behaving like mere men?' (1 Corinthians 3:3).

Christian growth is not a theoretical concept – it is an important part of our relationship with God. If you love someone you will want your relationship to develop. That is why Paul prays that we might be 'growing in the knowledge of God' (Colossians 1:10, NIV). Dick Lucas makes an interesting comment on this verse, he says 'just as we speak of "studying" to please our friends, so we need to "study" God's pleasure by searching out His likes and dislikes as He has revealed them.'[2] When a young couple first marry they find out all kinds of things they never knew about each other and it does not take too long to realise which of these discoveries leads to tensions between them. As they learn about these things, and work at their differences their relationship will grow. In the same way, as we read God's Word and prayerfully apply it to our lives we will change the things that displease Him and grow in our relationship.

Spiritual growth, then, is essential for living the Christian life. Let's go for growth!

God centred growth

When Breakfast Television was first broadcast in Britain, a man calling himself 'Mr. Motivator' used to spend five minutes each day demonstrating an exercise routine. His catch phrase was 'get motivated', which got right to the heart of the matter; you will never have the discipline for a daily regime of exercise if you have not got the motivation. This is true of spiritual growth, but before we 'get motivated' we had better make sure we have the right motives.

There is no doubt that spiritual growth has great benefits. It increases our joy, deepens our relationship with God, makes us more effective in our Christian lives and enables us to be more victorious in our battle against sin. These are huge incentives, but they are not the most important reasons as to why we should grow.

In the opening verse of Ephesians, Paul gives us a panoramic view of God's plan; pulling back the curtains of time he tells us about God's purposes which were established before the world was created.

'Just as He chose us in Him before the foundation of the world, that we should be holy and without blame before Him in love, having predestined us to adoption as sons by Jesus Christ to Himself, according to the good pleasure of His will, to the praise of the glory of His grace, by which He has made us accepted in the Beloved' (Ephesians 1:4-6).

Then he gives us a glimpse into the future, to tell us about God's ultimate purposes.

'In Him we have redemption through His blood, the forgiveness of sins, according to the riches of His grace which He made to abound toward us in all wisdom and prudence, having made known to us the mystery of His will, according to His good pleasure which He purposed in Himself, that in the dispensation of the fullness of the times He might gather together in one all things in Christ, both which are in heaven and which are on earth—in Him. In Him also we have obtained an inheritance, being predestined according to the purpose of Him who works all things according to the counsel of His will, that we who first trusted in Christ should be to the praise of His glory' (Ephesians 1:7-12).

He also speaks of the way in which the Holy Spirit has come to dwell within us and in doing so guarantees the final stage of our salvation.

'In Him you also trusted, after you heard the word of truth, the gospel of your salvation; in whom also, having believed, you were sealed with the Holy Spirit of promise, who is the guarantee of our inheritance until the redemption of the purchased possession, to the praise of His glory' (Ephesians 1:13-14).

Have you noticed a phrase that Paul uses repeatedly? In verses 6, 12 and 14 he tells us that these things are 'to the praise of His glory'. John Piper says: 'in each of these instances what is being expressed is God's goal. God elects, predestines and secures for one great ultimate purpose–that the glory of his grace might be praised forever and ever with white hot affection.'[3]

We usually think of growth in terms of what it does for us, but if we are going to understand it correctly we should concentrate on the glory it brings to God, and see the benefits as additional. In his classic book, '*The Pursuit of Holiness*', Jerry Bridges asks why we do not experience holiness in our day to day lives when it is so basic to the Christian life. He goes on to say that this is because 'our attitude toward sin is more self-centred than God-centred. We are more concerned about our own "victory" over sin than we are about the fact that our sins grieve the heart of God. We cannot tolerate failure in our struggle with sin chiefly because we are success-orientated, not because we know it is offensive to God.'[4] In the same way, our attitude towards spiritual growth can often be self-centred rather than God-centred.

Who does what?

There are times when we are like pendulums–swinging from one extreme to another! Some people put so much emphasis on the part we play in spiritual growth, that they become legalistic. These kind of people define growth in terms of 'do's' and 'don'ts'; if you read your Bible every day, go to Church every week and do not go to certain places, you will grow. But you've got to keep at it and give it everything you've got. Others tell us not to worry about what we can do; 'just let go and let God,' they tell us 'leave it all to Him.' But the Bible endorses neither extreme.

One of my favourite verses is Philippians 1:6 in which Paul says: 'being confident of this very thing, that He who has begun a good work in you will complete it until the day of Jesus Christ.' I often read this verse to people who are struggling with the Christian life, and it also shapes the way I pray for my Church, family, and friends. However, encouraging this is, it does not give us an excuse to sit back and expect God to do everything for us. Later on in Philippians we are told to: 'work out (our) own salvation with fear and trembling' and we must do this because 'it is God who works in (us) both to will and to do for His good pleasure' (Philippians 2:12-13). This is the balance which the New Testament gives us; we 'work out what God has worked in'.

Christian growth is started and sustained by God; 1 Corinthians 3:7 says 'neither he who plants nor he who waters is anything, but only God who makes things grow' (NIV). However, it is not automatic, we must make a response. This involves us reading and obeying God's Word (1 Peter 2:2; Hebrews 5:11-14), committing ourselves to a local Church (Ephesians 5:15-21), and making personal choices that will keep our lives in line with God's Word.

Go for growth!

Have you met people who seem to spend their lives apologising; 'I only have a low rank in my office—what kind of effect can I have on the people I work with?' 'We are only a little fellowship—how could we possibly reach our neighbourhood.' A lot of the time these are not really apologies—they're excuses! We can do the same kind of thing when we talk about spiritual growth. We bemoan the fact that we might not be particularly strong Christians, or that our Bible knowledge is not what it should be, or that we are not as effective as we would like to be; when we should be doing something to change these things. We have got to replace defeatist attitude with dynamic Christian living, and the Word of God should shape our approach to this. We can begin to do so by having an understanding of the work God is doing in our lives.

God at work!

Have you ever got lost, stopped your car to ask for directions and ended up even more confused? 'Can you tell me how to get to Southend Pier?' you ask a friendly looking local. 'Certainly,' he says with a trace of a frown on his face. 'Just continue in the direction you're going, look out for a big church and then turn right down the second, or third turning and it will be somewhere around there.' As helpful as that person has tried to be, he has not made things any clearer, in fact, if anything you are less clear! The same thing can happen when Christians talk about spiritual growth; they describe it in such a vague way that few people understand what it is. Growth is often spoken about as if it was something that automatically happens to us, or which is merely outward, or so spiritual that it cannot possibly be monitored.

The Bible, however, speaks of growth in a very specific way. It presents an overall goal – perfection! In the Sermon on the Mount, Jesus said: 'you shall be perfect, just as your Father in heaven is perfect' (Matthew 5:48). Paul looks forward to the time when 'we [the Church] all come to the unity of the faith and of the knowledge of the Son of God, to a perfect man, to the measure of the stature of the fullness of Christ' (Ephesians 4:13). And when James teaches us how to grow through our trials he tells us to: 'let patience have its perfect work, that (we) may be perfect and complete, lacking nothing' (James 1:4). In each of these verses the word translated 'perfect' emphasises wholeness or completeness. It can also be used in a natural sense to speak of a person becoming 'full grown' or 'mature', but here it speaks of spiritual maturity.

Once we have looked at the goal we can turn our attention to the grounds for spiritual growth, and this rests in two areas, which are given to us in 2 Peter 3:18: 'grow in the grace and knowledge of our Lord and Saviour Jesus Christ.'

The first area is grace. While the explanation of grace as 'the unmerited favour of God' is true, the New Testament provides us with a much richer understanding. 'Grace' speaks of the way in which God accepts us, even though we are incapable of earning His favour. It calls us to have total dependence upon the work that Christ has done in our lives, and upon the power of the Holy Spirit. In the introductory verses of his Gospel, John tells us: 'of [Christ's] fullness we have all received, and grace for grace' (John 1:16). In Acts we are told: 'great grace was upon' the Early Church (Acts 4:33). Paul writes to the Corinthians, spelling out the evidences of God's grace saying: 'I thank my God always concerning you for the grace of God which was given to you by Christ Jesus, that you were enriched in everything by Him in all utterance and all knowledge,' (1 Corinthians 1:4-5). And Ephesians declares: 'by grace (we) have been saved through faith' (Ephesians 2:8).

The second area is 'knowledge of our Lord and Savior Jesus Christ'. This is more than knowing about Christ; it involves a relationship with Him. Commenting on this verse Michael Green says: 'it is through personal encounter with Jesus as Saviour and Lord that the Christian life begins. It is through constant contact with Him ... that Christian character develops.'[5] This is the essence of Christianity; it is not a religion, but a living relationship with Christ. Jesus told the disciples they were His friends (John 15.14). James presents Abraham as our role model and says that his faith made him 'a friend of God' (James 2:23). And John says: 'our fellowship is with the Father and with His Son Jesus Christ' (1 John 1:3).

While the grounds of spiritual growth are grace and knowledge of Christ, it is brought about as we live for Him. When Paul writes to the Christians at Colosse he tells them of his prayer, that they will be filled 'with the knowledge of His will through all spiritual wisdom and understanding.' Then he tells them he is praying for this in order that they may 'live a life worthy of the Lord and may please him in every way: bearing fruit in every good work, growing in the knowledge of God,' (Colossians 1:9-10 NIV). Of course, this does not mean we have to try and make ourselves worthy of acceptance by Christ – He accepts us as we are. It means that our lives are consistent with our relationship with Him. Ephesians 4:1 has the same challenge: 'I, therefore, the prisoner of the Lord, beseech you to walk worthy of the calling with which you were called.' And in Philippians we are called to 'let (our) conduct be worthy of the gospel of Christ' (Philippians 1:27).

If we are going to live for Christ, our aim must be to please God 'in every way,' (Colossians 1:10). This will be a useful tool to help us make sure we are on the path to growth. We can stand back, look at what we have been, thinking, saying, and doing and ask ourselves a simple question–'am I pleasing God?' If the answer is 'no' then we must do something about it, and as we make the changes which are necessary we will be doing something to increase our growth rate.

An expert hand

It is fascinating to watch a craftsman at work. It can be captivating to observe his steadiness of hand and precision of movement. The Bible tells us that we are: 'God's workmanship' (Ephesians 2:10). He has begun a work in us, He is in the process of continuing that work, and He will 'complete it until the day of Jesus Christ' (Philippians 1:6). We are going to spend some time considering this.

Something from nothing

No matter how skilful a human craftsman may be he cannot create a masterpiece from poor material—but God is able to make something from nothing! In Ephesians 2 Paul tells us how He does this with us:

'And you He made alive, who were dead in trespasses and sins, in which you once walked according to the course of this world, according to the prince of the power of the air, the spirit who now works in the sons of disobedience, among whom also we all once conducted ourselves in the lusts of our flesh, fulfilling the desires of the flesh and of the mind, and were by nature children of wrath, just as the others. But God, who is rich in mercy, because of His great love with which He loved us, even when we were dead in trespasses, made us alive together with Christ (by grace you have been saved), and raised us up together, and made us sit together in the heavenly places in Christ Jesus, that in the ages to come He might show the exceeding riches of His grace in His kindness toward us in Christ Jesus. For by grace you have been saved through faith, and that not of yourselves; it is the gift of God, not of works, lest anyone should boast. For we are His workmanship, created in Christ Jesus for good works, which God prepared beforehand that we should walk in them.' (Ephesians 2:1-10).

Paul begins with the bad news, describing our condition before we came to Christ.

First, we were 'dead in trespasses and sins in which (we) once walked according to the course of this world.' Although we had the ability to eat, drink, sleep and breathe, we were spiritually dead. If that seems a contradiction in terms, let me give you an illustration, which will explain this. A man stops off on the way home from work to buy his wife some flowers. When he arrives he decides to knock at the door so that he can greet his wife by giving her the flowers. 'Oh how lovely,' she says 'I'll go and put them in water.' A few days later their scent has disappeared, their colour faded and their leaves have withered – why? Because, pretty as they might be, they were dead; they had been cut off from their source of life. They went through the motions of living, but it was only a matter of time before they withered and died. We were like those flowers. We went through all the motions of living, but our sin had cut us off from God.

Secondly, we were on the road to ruin. We lived 'according to the course of this world'- rejecting God's laws and following the world's standards and ideals. But, as we did so something else was going on. We were following the 'prince of the power of the air, the spirit who now works in the sons of disobedience.' When we 'conducted ourselves in the lusts of our flesh, fulfilling the desires of the flesh and of the mind' we thought we were following our own ambitions and desires, but we were actually doing the very things Satan wanted us to!

Thirdly, we 'were by nature children of wrath.' Our sin and godlessness brought us under the certain prospect of eternal punishment. Many people find this hard to take. 'How can you talk about the love of God one minute and the wrath of God the next?' They say, 'a loving God cannot be a condemning God!' They fail to understand that He is also a holy God—He is separate, sinless, pure and just. A holy God hates sin and a just God must punish it; if he did not he would be acting inconsistently with his holiness and His justice.

That is the material the master craftsman has to work with; what is He able to do with it? It can be summed up in the statement: 'you have been saved' (Ephesians 2:8). This is a word we take for granted, but it is one of the most powerful in the New Testament. In some instances it is used to speak of the way in which someone has been rescued from physical danger—such as a storm at sea (Acts 27:20,31). But it usually speaks about the way in which God, in Christ, has rescued us from the powers of sin, death, and Satan, and the prospect of His wrath.

God displays His character in this work. After setting out the stark truth about the kind of people we were before we came to Christ, Paul changes course with two simple, yet powerful words 'but God,' which contrasts our hopeless condition with God's workmanship. He tells us that God is 'rich in mercy', he speaks of God's 'great love with which He loved us,' and he talks of the grace of God by which 'we have been saved.'

God's work also unites us with Christ. We can see this in the way in which Paul links it with three events in Christ's work. His resurrection - 'God…made us alive together with Christ' (Ephesians 2:5). His ascension to heaven—'and raised us up together' (Ephesians 2:5). And His heavenly rule (which is often called His session)—'and made us sit together in the heavenly places in Christ Jesus' (Ephesians 2:6). But how can we be united with Christ 'in the heavenly places' when we still live on earth? This is a term that has been used in Ephesians several times to speak of the supernatural realm (see 1:3, 3:10, 6:12). It is where Satan is active and Christ rules. John Stott describes it as 'the unseen world of spiritual reality where the principalities and powers operate and in which Christ reigns supreme.'[6]

The result of this work will be 'that in the ages to come He might show the exceeding riches of His grace in His kindness toward us in Christ Jesus'. And our part in this has been carefully prepared for us. 'For we are His workmanship, created in Christ Jesus for good works, which God prepared beforehand that we should walk in them.' It is a work of God from start to finish!

The master plan

If you have ever admired a magnificent building, you will know that it would not have been constructed in a haphazard way. The work began in the architects' drawing room a long time before the builders arrived. Similarly, God's work in us began with a design, and we will follow it through in this chapter.

Chosen by God

If there is one word that is capable of raising the temperature of a discussion amongst Christians it is 'election.' But, whether we like it or not, it is used in the Bible. When Paul writes to the Christians at Thessolonica telling them of the way he gives thanks for them he speaks of their 'election by God' (1 Thessalonians 1:4). In Titus 1:1 he describes himself as 'a bond-servant of God and an apostle of Jesus Christ, according to the faith of God's elect.' And in 2 Timothy 2:10 he says ' I endure all things for the sake of the elect, that they also may obtain the salvation which is in Christ Jesus with eternal glory.' Jesus used the word too, He spoke of His return in terms of gathering 'His elect from the four winds, from the farthest part of earth to the farthest part of heaven. (Mark 13:27). And in the closing days of His ministry He told the disciples: 'You did not choose Me, but I chose you and appointed you that you should go and bear fruit,' (John 15:16).

Now we have established that 'election' is a Biblical word, we can think about its meaning and relevance to our spiritual growth. J. I. Packer says that the verb 'elect' or 'choose,' 'expresses the idea of picking out, or selecting, something or someone from a number of available alternatives...we read in both Testaments of God choosing out men for Himself.'[7] What does the Bible tell us about it? First, we have been chosen 'in Christ' (Ephesians 1:4). This means that God's choice is made effective through Jesus' death and resurrection. Secondly, we have been chosen 'for salvation (2 Thessalonians 2:13). Thirdly, we have been chosen to live a holy life (2 Timothy 1:9). However, it is important to remember that we have not been chosen because we are capable of living such a life, but because God, in His mercy, has saved us and has 'given us all things that pertain to life and godliness' (2 Peter 1:3). Thirdly, we were chosen 'before the foundation of the world' (Ephesians 1:4).

You might look at this and say 'well, if God has done all this for me, there is not much I need to be doing' but you could not be further from the truth. The New Testament uses election to spur us into action. In Colossians we are told 'as the elect of God' to 'put on tender mercies, kindness, humility, meekness, longsuffering' (Colossians 3:12). Peter says we must 'make our call and election sure' (2 Peter 1:10). Election acts as an incentive to spiritual growth.

New lives for old!

Shortly after I became a Christian I was very moved by the story of Charles Colson, who had been in prison on charges related to the Watergate scandal in the United States. Colson wrote a powerful book describing how he became a Christian, entitled 'Born again'; this title seemed to say everything about the work God had done in his life. Although our society has abused this term we shouldn't be afraid of using it, because it is in the Bible, and it first came from Jesus. 'I tell you the truth,' He said 'no-one can see the kingdom of God unless he is born again' (John 3:3 NIV). The phrase used by Jesus literally means 'born from above', and it describes the new birth which God brings about when a person first turns to Christ. This marks the very beginning of the process of spiritual growth. John talks about this in the opening verses of his Gospel when he says: 'as many as received (Christ), to them He gave the right to become children of God, to those who believe in His name: who were born, not of blood, nor of the will of the flesh, nor of the will of man, but of God' (John 1:12-13). And Peter says God has given us 'new birth into a living hope through the resurrection of Jesus Christ from the dead,' (1 Peter 1:3 NIV).

New birth is a work of the Father, Son and Holy Spirit. It is a work of God the Father (John 1:13, 1 Peter 1:3), who has made us 'alive together' with Christ (Ephesians 2:5, Colossians 2:13). It is only possible because Jesus has taken our punishment upon Himself (1 Peter 2:24). And it is brought about by 'the washing of regeneration and renewing of the Holy Spirit,' (Titus 3:5).

If you have a parade of shops near to your home you have probably noticed one or two shops that are complete eyesores. The stock is out of date, the paint is peeling off and the window frames are going rotten. Then, everything changes. Decorators give the front of the shop a new look, the old sign is taken down and a new one is put in its place, the shelves are stocked properly and the people who serve are more helpful. What has happened? It can all be explained by a notice hanging in the shop window: 'under new management.' A new owner has taken charge and changed it from top to bottom. New birth has the same effect on our lives—God brings about a thorough change. We are a 'new creation' (2 Corinthians 5:17) and 'partakers of the divine nature' (2 Peter 1:4). We will acquire a hatred of sin (1 John 3:9; 5:18) and be given victory over the world (1 John 5:4). We are given a new nature which is 'created to be like God in true righteousness and holiness' (Ephesians 4:24 NIV) and is 'being renewed in knowledge in the image of its Creator' (Colossians 3:10 NIV). Although our new birth is a 'one off' event it begins a process which continues as we grow.

The great conclusion

Is there ever a time when we stop growing? There is, and it comes as God brings His work within us to its great conclusion at the final resurrection. The resurrection has always been a source of great certainty and comfort to Christians. Paul once spoke of a very difficult time when he and his colleagues were in Ephesus. They were 'burdened beyond measure, above strength, so that (they) despaired of life itself.' But, reflecting on the lessons learned he went on to say that they had learned not to trust in themselves 'but in God who raises from the dead,' (2 Corinthians 1:8-9). Paul was not just talking about the resurrection of Jesus—he was looking forward to an event that is a natural progression from this—the day when every believer will be totally transformed by the power of resurrection.

There is nothing uncertain about this because it is linked with Jesus' resurrection. In 1 Corinthians 15 Paul sets out the order of events: 'each one in his own order, Christ the firstfruits, afterward those who are Christ's at His coming' (1 Corinthians 15:23). The 'firstfruits' were the initial instalment of harvest, which was dedicated to God and guaranteed full harvest to be gathered in. Paul uses this word to tell us that we can be certain about the resurrection to come because Christ has been already raised from the dead.

What will happen when this great day finally arrives? We are given a concise description of what is going to take place in 1 Thessalonians chapter 4. First, 'the Lord Himself will descend from heaven.' Secondly, Christians who have already died will be raised from the dead. And thirdly, those of us who will still be alive will 'be caught up together with them in the clouds to meet the Lord in the air' (1 Thessalonians 4:17) and we will have resurrection bodies.

What will these bodies be like? They will be physical, but they will be transformed and suited to a heavenly existence. Although it is 'sown a natural body, it is raised a spiritual body' (1 Corinthians 15:42-44). The word 'spiritual' speaks of it as being consistent with the character and activity of the Holy Spirit. Wayne Grudem says that 'it is not at all "non physical." But is a physical body raised to the degree of perfection for which God originally intended it to be.[8]'

The final question we need to face is what happens to us between death and resurrection? The Bible gives us an unequivocal answer—we go to be with the Lord! Jesus told the dying thief 'today you will be with me in paradise' (Luke 23:43). Paul said 'we .. would prefer to be away from the body and at home with the Lord. (2 Corinthians 5:8 NIV). When he wrestled with the possibility of pardon or execution from Caesar he told the Christians at Phillipi that to 'depart and be with Christ' was 'far better' (Philippians 1:23). And the writer to the Hebrews talks about heavenly worship where there are 'the spirits of just men made perfect' (Hebrews 12:23). This is called the 'intermediate state' because, wonderful as it is, the best is yet to come when God brings His plan to its great conclusion at the final resurrection.

The master craftsman knows exactly what He is doing; He has a plan, which He will complete, and we need to understand spiritual growth in this context.

The master builder

Saying goodbye to someone you have been close to can be very painful, especially when you are apprehensive about what might happen to them after you have left. This was how Paul felt when he said farewell to the Elders of the Church at Ephesus. After leading them to Christ, teaching them, establishing their Church, and expanding their mission, he set sail for Jerusalem. Paul was not concerned for himself; he was ready to face any hardship that came his way as he spread the Gospel. 'The Holy Spirit testifies in every city, saying that chains and tribulations await me,' he said. 'But none of these things move me; nor do I count my life dear to myself, so that I may finish my race with joy, and the ministry which I received from the Lord Jesus, to testify to the gospel of the grace of God,' (Acts 20:23-24). His greatest concern was the 'wolves' who were going to try and divide the Church. 'From among yourselves men will rise up, speaking perverse things, to draw away the disciples after themselves. Therefore watch, and remember that for three years I did not cease to warn everyone night and day with tears,' (Acts 20:29-31). Fearful as he was, Paul was confident that the Word of God was sufficient to counter this danger, and bring about spiritual growth. 'So now, brethren, I commend you to God and to the word of His grace, which is able to build you up and give you an inheritance among all those who are sanctified,' (Acts 20:32).

Today, there are many books, seminars, and teaching materials available from people who have seen a lot of growth in their churches. Each person emphasises a particular aspect or method, which is often very helpful. But Paul, the greatest Church planter of all time, emphasised the Word of God.' He said that 'faith comes by hearing, and hearing by the word of God. (Romans 10:17). He told Timothy to 'preach the Word' (2 Timothy 4:2). He called it 'the sword of the Spirit' (Ephesians 6:17). And he said that 'all Scripture is given by inspiration of God, and is profitable for doctrine, for reproof, for correction, for instruction in righteousness,' (2 Timothy 3:16). If the Word was central to the man who helped so many Christians to grow, we should regard it as one of the most important things needed to develop our relationship with Christ.

The Word played an important part in the process of our new birth. The New Testament tells us that we have 'been born again, not of corruptible seed but incorruptible, through the word of God which lives and abides forever, (1 Peter 1:23). And it is also crucial for spiritual growth. Peter goes on to say 'as newborn babes, desire the pure milk of the word, that you may grow thereby,' (1 Peter 2:2).

Since the Word plays such a significant role, it must occupy an important place in our lives. We should set aside time each day to spend with God, read His Word, and pray about the challenges it gives to us. We must familiarise ourselves with it. As a young Christian I found the Navigators 'Topical Memory System' extremely helpful. Each week I memorised several verses from the Bible under topics relevant to Christian growth, and by the time I finished I found that I had a wealth of scripture at my fingertips, which helped enormously.

Finally, we must put the Word into practice. James warns us against people who hear the Word, but do not do anything about it: 'Be doers of the word, and not hearers only, deceiving yourselves. For if anyone is a hearer of the word and not a doer, he is like a man observing his natural face in a mirror; for he observes himself, goes away, and immediately forgets what kind of man he was. But he who looks into the perfect law of liberty and continues in it, and is not a forgetful hearer but a doer of the work, this one will be blessed in what he does,' (James 1:22-25). Our true response to God's Word will be shown in our willingness to obey it.

Spiritual growth is all about 'building yourself up in your most holy faith' (Jude 20), and the Word of God is the master builder.

The master tool

It had been an exhausting, emotional evening. Thirteen men had shared a meal together; their host told them that one of the people sitting around the table was going to defect to their enemies and give away information that would lead to his death. After the traitor had slipped out into the night the host told the remaining eleven he was going away, and that they could not come with Him. They found this hard to understand; after all they had been with Him for three action-packed years, why did he want to go off on his own now? One of them even said that he would follow him anywhere, even if he were to die in the process. After the meal they went to a secluded spot, and Jesus, who had hosted the meal, asked them to stay awake and keep Him company while He prayed.

Although He spent time praying about the ordeal laying ahead of Him, much of Jesus' prayer was taken up with His future followers (John 17:20). He asked His Father to sanctify us 'in truth', adding 'your Word is truth' (John 17:18).

There was Jesus, anticipating the agony of the Cross, distressed because a close friend had betrayed Him (John 13:21), and facing the prospect of being separated from His Father for the first time in eternity. What was on His mind? The result of the work He was about to do, people like you and I, forgiven and 'sanctified' by God.

What's in a word?
There is a tendency today to shy away from a 'theological' word like 'sanctification'. This is a great pity, because it was something Jesus asked His Father to do for us, and it is an essential part of spiritual growth. That is why we are going to spend some time defining the meaning of the word.

Although it may sound a bit daunting 'sanctification' is very straight forward—it means 'to be set apart'. It is used to talk about the way we are set apart to God (Acts 20:32), and set apart from the 'evil desires' that used to drive us before we were Christians (1 Thessalonians 4:3). In the Old Testament it speaks about the way in which a person, or an object would be set apart from everyday life and put to service for God; particularly in the Temple.

We become 'sanctified' as we grow to be more like Jesus, and reflect His likeness to all around us. Imagine a craftsman who goes into the depths of a forest and cuts some wood. He takes it to his workshop where he makes it into a bowl which he is going to give as a present. He realises it will be put on someone's kitchen table and used day in, day out, but he is a master craftsman, so he takes his time and makes an exquisite object. When he finishes, he gives it to someone who he will not see for a long time, so that they can remember him by it. As expected, the bowl gets used each day, but each time it is picked up the person thinks of the craftsman and admires his skill. That is what God is doing with us. He takes us, sets us apart, works on us and makes us more like Jesus, so that people appreciate His work, and think about Him. Of course, God does not hide us away while He's doing this; it is all done in the rough and tumble of life!

A Matter of balance

Sanctification is a work of God. Jude tells us so in the opening verses of his letter when he says we are 'sanctified by God the Father, and preserved in Jesus Christ' (Jude 1:1). And Paul draws first Thessalonians to a close with a prayer that God will completely sanctify us (1 Thessalonians 5:23). God brings this about through His Holy Spirit, who dwells in us (1 Corinthians 7:19), making us more like Jesus (Colossians 3:10). And through His Word which 'is able to build us up and give us an inheritance among all those who are sanctified' (Acts 20:32).

Although it is God's work, we have a role to play. Paul tells us to 'work out our own salvation with fear and trembling', reminding us that God is working in us (Philippians 2:12-13). And Hebrews urges us to 'strive for holiness' (Hebrews 12:14 NIV). God has begun the work, and He will complete it; but there are some things we must do. It is our responsibility to resist temptation (1Corinthians 10:13), obey the Word (1 Peter 1:22), and refuse to have anything to do with immorality (1 Corinthians 6:18). And we have no excuse, because God's 'divine power has given to us all things that pertain to life and godliness' (2 Peter 1:3).

If you have had an operation you will know that recovery can be a painstaking process. It begins with the surgeon who operates, then no sooner have you begun to learn to live with your aches and pains when a physiotherapist arrives to help you to recover. He or she will set you exercises, and help you to get back on your feet again. You could not be made well without the surgeon, and you could not recover without the physiotherapist; but you will have to put some work in too. Sanctification is like that; God works in us, His Word shows us how we are to live, and the Holy Spirit is within us giving us everything we need to obey it. But He expects us to put it into practice.

Time scale

It was the lesson we had all been dreading. Our teacher, a former Royal Marine, ran the class like a battalion. We had hardly sat down and exchanged nervous glances when he burst into the room: 'Right!' he said, at the top of his voice, 'it's time to talk about your work.' This was not a very promising start; he wore a frown on his face, and looked around the room. 'Who is going to start then?' he said, with a menacing tone. Every head dipped, and no hands went up, so he called someone to come out to the front. He picked up the essay, glanced through it and, to our amazement, he smiled. 'A good piece of work,' he said, 'it has three essential things—a beginning, a middle, and an end.'

Sanctification is not instant, it takes time and, like the essay praised by my teacher; it has a beginning, a middle, and an end. The work began when God gave us new life. A religious teacher once came to see Jesus: leaving his house under the cover of darkness, so that no-one saw him make his journey. He began by complimenting Jesus: 'I know you are a teacher who has been sent to us from God. After all, no-one could do the kind of miracles we have seen at your hand if God was not with him!' Jesus was not moved by the compliment, He got straight to the issue this man had to face: 'You will not be able to see the Kingdom of God unless you are born again.'[9] The teacher shook his head, and tried to work out what Jesus was saying, it did not seem to make sense. 'You cannot be saying that I need to go back into my mother's womb so that I go through the experience of birth all over again!' he said. Jesus persisted, and spelt out exactly what He meant, He told him that He was not talking about natural birth, but spiritual birth. 'That which is born of the flesh is flesh, and that which is born of the Spirit is spirit' (John 3:6). The term 'born again' is often misused in the world around us, but we must never forget what an important thing it describes. God's Spirit has worked within us to give us new life. He has 'begotten us again to a living hope' (1 Peter 1:3), and has 'saved us, through the washing of regeneration and renewing of the Holy Spirit' (Titus 3:5).

Are you one of those people who start something with a burst of enthusiasm, but run out of steam halfway through? If you are, you probably have a list of unfinished jobs. I'm glad to say God is not like that; He finishes His work. As a Pastor I speak to a lot of people who are discouraged about their Christian life. I listen to what they have to say, open my Bible, and often encourage them with this great verse: 'He who has begun a good work in you will carry it on to completion until the day of Jesus Christ' (Philippians 1:6 NIV). There are going to be times when we make mistakes and let the Lord down. But He will not give up on us, because He has promised to finish what He has started. In fact, He will even use our failures to teach us some important lessons. We'll be thinking about this later on in the book.

Is there a time when we can sit back satisfied in the knowledge that God has finished His work? In the past there have been people who thought so. They spoke about a condition of 'sinless perfection' when our sanctification is complete. A famous preacher was once speaking at a conference where another speaker confidently declared that he had reached this condition. Rather than contradict him, he decided to put it to the test. So, the next morning they sat down to breakfast, and exchanged greetings. The preacher got up from his seat, picked up a jug of milk and poured it over the man's head. His reaction was far from perfect, and the preacher wrote in his diary 'I tested his doctrine and proved it to be false'!

When can we look forward to the final stage of God's work? The answer is in the encouraging verse from Philippians we have already thought about – 'on the day of Christ Jesus.' Which is when Jesus returns and 'will transform our lowly body that it may be conformed to His glorious body' (Philippians 3:21).

If you spend a lot of time staring at a computer screen or reading, your eyes will get sore and when you ask your Optician's advice he or she will encourage you to look up every so often and focus on a distant object.

Sometimes the process of spiritual growth can be painful and slow. One effective way to counter this would be to look up at the big picture we have just thought about. This will motivate us to keep going. That is why, in 1 Thessalonians, after telling us about the return of the Lord Jesus, which brings God's plan into completion, Paul prays for our sanctification. 'May the God of peace Himself sanctify you completely' so for your 'whole spirit, soul, and body be preserved blameless at the coming of our Lord Jesus Christ,' (1 Thessalonians 5:23).

Results to rejoice in

Although God's work in us will not be finished until we get to heaven, there are many benefits we will enjoy in this life. There will be a sense of joy as we progress on in our Christian life. We will be more focussed on heaven and less on earth. We will reflect Christ and we will be more effective in telling other people the good news. Sanctification is the master tool, and we will not grow without it!

The perfect pattern

Each day I shut myself in a room, got out my guitar, tuned up, and put every ounce of concentration into the piece of music I wanted to learn. In the first few days I stumbled through, struggling to translate the notes on the page into sounds. But day by day it became more familiar and easier to manage, until I had finally mastered it—just in time for my lesson! 'What have you got for me this week?' asked my teacher. I pulled out the music, put it on the stand and looked round to see him give a nod of approval. 'Let us hear it then,' he said with expectancy, and I gave it everything I had. As the last note faded away I looked round to see a wistful look on his face. He began by talking about the things he liked about the performance and then pointed out the areas needing more work. 'I'll tell you what,' he said, as he picked up a tape 'let us hear how the master plays it.' For the next few minutes we followed the music to a recording of a well-known guitarist. 'Aim at that,' my teacher said, 'and you cannot go wrong.'

Whether it is music, athletics, soccer, or tennis, we need a role model. This gives us something to aim for and work towards, and spiritual growth is no exception. Paul encouraged the Christians at Corinth to follow his example, as he followed Christ's (1 Corinthians 11:1), and he told a young Pastor, called Timothy, to 'be an example to the believers in word, in conduct, in love, in spirit, in faith, in purity' (1 Timothy 4:12). But the perfect pattern can only be found in Jesus, and the Bible tells us that as we grow, we become more like Him (Colossians 3:10, Ephesians 4:24, 1 Corinthians 3:18). That is why we are going to spend some time thinking about the example he sets for us.

Tempted yet triumphant

For thirty years Jesus had lived in Nazareth, and much of His time had been spent in Joseph's workshop, but the time had come for His public work to begin and it started dramatically! Jesus' cousin, John, had already begun his ministry. He went to the desert, where crowds of people came to hear him announcing that God was about to do a new thing, and he called them to prepare for this by turning from their sins. He spent a lot of his time baptising people in the river Jordan, and many of them started to speculate that he might be the new King promised by God through the Prophets. John quickly put a stop to this idea and told them he was not the Messiah. He could only baptise people in the water, but the one who was coming would do a spiritual work, which would change their lives.

Finally, the person he had been telling them about arrived—it was Jesus, and He asked John to baptise Him! 'I should not be baptising you,' protested John, 'you should baptise me!' 'No,' insisted Jesus 'this is the right thing to do.' John led Jesus to the river, and immersed Him in the water, and as Jesus emerged an incredible thing happened. The Holy Spirit took the form of a dove and rested on Him, and God the Father spoke saying 'this is my Son, who I love, and who I am pleased with' (Luke 3:22).

The scene suddenly moved from excitement to endurance. The Holy Spirit led Jesus into the desert where He fasted. After forty days without food Jesus' stamina would have been stretched to the limit, and it was at this point that Satan tempted Him. Trying to sow doubt in His mind, and prey on his physical weakness Satan began with the most pressing human need. 'If you are the Son of God, command this stone to become bread' (Luke 4:3). This was very subtle; after forty days without food the process of starvation would have started, so this is more than a question of satisfying a human desire, it is about life and death. In effect Satan was saying 'if you are God's Son, with a task to perform and a ministry to fulfil, do not you think you had better eat something. Why do not you use your powers to help you?' And behind his words was a disguised message that if God the Father was not caring for Him, He had better take care of Himself. Jesus instantly responded by quoting the Bible. 'It is written, "man shall not live by bread alone but by every Word of God"' (Luke 4:4).

Satan persisted, and drew Jesus' attention to all the Kingdoms of the world, promising to give Him authority over them and greatness. This was going to belong to Jesus after He had risen and ascended; but Satan was offering them now without the need to suffer. Jesus, however, kept His eye on His Father and His mind on the Word. 'Get behind Me, Satan! For it is written, "You shall worship the Lord your God, and Him only you shall serve"' (Luke 4:8).

Satan's next wave of attack was the most dramatic. He drew Jesus' attention to the highest point of the temple in Jerusalem, which towered over a four hundred and fifty-foot drop. 'If you are the Son of God, throw yourself down from here,' he said, and then had the audacity to quote the Bible: 'For it is written: "He shall give His angels charge over you, To keep you,"', and, "In their hands they shall bear you up, Lest you dash your foot against a stone" (Luke 4:10-11). Realising Satan was twisting scripture, Jesus pointed out another verse that said "You shall not tempt the Lord your God" (Luke 4:12).

The Bible tells us that Jesus has been 'in all points tempted as we are, yet without sin' (Hebrews 4:15). And His example here shows us that He was able to resist it by His grasp of the Word.

When I went to fairs as a child I used to like the 'lucky dip.' I would pay my money, put my hand in the bag, and take out whatever I had picked. Some people treat the Bible like that! They grab hold of any promise that attracts them, without understanding what it means in the context or against the background of the wider picture given to us in the Bible. It is interesting that in the last temptation Satan tried to twist the Bible and misquote a verse. If we are going to grow through resisting temptation we will need to learn how to handle the Bible properly.

Obedient to death

Another characteristic we can see in Jesus is His obedience to the Father. When Jesus was a boy His parents travelled from Nazareth to Jerusalem to take him to the Temple. After they had got a little way into their journey home they realised that He was not with them. They turned round, and retraced their steps back to Jerusalem where they found Him sitting with the Teachers in the Temple courts. When Mary told Him how worried they had been Jesus said: 'did not you know that I would be about my Father's business?' (Luke 2:49). During His ministry Jesus said: 'my food is to do the will of Him who sent Me, and to finish His work' (John 4:34). He also said he would do this work 'while it is day' (John 9:3) and described Himself as a servant (Mark 10:45), and when He prayed in Gethsemene He said: 'I have finished the work which you have given me to do' (John 17:4). Jesus, the perfect man, showed complete obedience to His Father and tells us to do the same. 'If you keep my commandments, you will abide in my love, just as I have kept my Father's commandments and abide in His love' (John 15:10).

Committed to the core

The road was dusty, the sun was high, and the atmosphere was tense. Jesus and the disciples were on their way to a city they had visited before, but this journey was different. Jesus told them that when they got to Jerusalem He was going to be betrayed, given into the hands of His enemies, and executed. The Disciples could not understand this; what purpose could there be in humiliation and pain, and how could this possibly fit in with Jesus' mission? So they did not give it much thought, in fact immediately after Jesus had spoken about this, the mother of two disciples asked Him if her two sons could be given the honour of sitting either side of Him in heaven. Jesus, however, 'steadfastly set His face to go to Jerusalem' (Luke 9:51).

A few days later He knelt in a garden, wrapped up in prayer. Jesus' betrayer had struck a bargain with His enemies; His arrest was imminent and His execution would happen within twenty-four hours. Jesus' praying was so intense that He sweated blood (Luke 22:44). Using an Aramaic word to reflect His intimate relationship with the Father together with a term from the Old Testament which spoke of judgement, Jesus said 'Abba, Father, all things are possible for you. Take this cup from me' (Mark 14:36).

He was not reluctant to die on the cross—He was facing up to the trauma which lay ahead. Jesus, the perfect man, was going to be judged for the sins of the world. There was no other way, so He closed His prayer by expressing His commitment: 'nevertheless not what I will, but what you want' (Mark 14:36). Then He got up and, finding His disciples fast asleep, said 'are you still sleeping and resting? It is enough! The hour has come; behold, the Son of Man is being betrayed into the hands of sinners. Rise, let us be going. See, My betrayer is at hand' (Mark 14:41-42). Jesus had talked about his death in terms of his 'hour' before. The hour had now come and He was ready to face it, because He was committed to the core.

As a Pastor, I hear lots of people telling me about the day they made 'a commitment to Christ', but the real test is when God calls us to do something we do not find very attractive. Jesus did not find the cross a pleasant prospect, the Bible tells us 'He endured the cross despising the shame' (Hebrews 12:2), but He was able to see it through because of His commitment. The next time you have to do something you do not want to, follow Jesus' example; put your own interests last and God's purposes first and you will find your growth rate increasing!

Perfect priorities

There was one name that was guaranteed to gather crowds and generate excitement - 'Jesus'. People flocked to meet Him. Some wanted to be healed, and others came to listen to Him speak, but everyone wanted contact with Him. They would go without meals, brave the heat, and go to the most incredible lengths to bring their needs to His attention. One group of men actually cut a hole in the roof of a house so that they could lower their bed-ridden friend in front of Him!

Many people would see such popularity as a mark of success. But Jesus did not. His priority was not to raise His profile, or to make a name for Himself, but to glorify His Father (John 12:38). Ultimately, He achieved this on the cross (John 13:31-32).

The Apostle John had the difficult task of warning churches about a troublesome man called Diotrephes who 'loves to be first' (3 John 7 NIV). Sadly this description can fit many Christians we meet today. They seek attention, and love being out the front, but they are reluctant to serve in the background. I knew someone who was very keen to have the post of 'administrator' in his Church. But when his Pastor asked him to do some paperwork for him he refused. He wanted to be someone, but he did not want to do anything! If he wanted to grow he would need to change his priorities.

Jesus said 'by this My Father is glorified, that you bear much fruit' (John 15:8) and we do so by living in a way that brings honour to God. This is certainly costly, but it should not be difficult as we 'are being transformed into [Christ's] likeness with ever-increasing glory, which comes from the Lord, who is the Spirit'. (2 Corinthians 3:18 NIV). The next time you find yourself talking to an awkward person or faced with a difficult situation, stop and think how you could glorify God and then get on and do it in the power He has given you.

Total trust

A historian once said that crucifixion: 'is the most barbaric death that man has ever devised to take vengeance on his fellow man.' In addition to His agony and separation from the Father, Jesus' ears were ringing with the sound of taunts from the people around Him. Peter tells us that instead of retaliating, Jesus 'committed Himself to Him who judges righteously' and we are urged to follow His example when we are faced with injustices, because if we take it patiently it is 'commendable before God' (1 Peter 3:21-22).

When we are under pressure, or being accused of something we have not done our natural reaction is to retaliate and defend ourselves. But if we were to stop, think, and follow Jesus' example we will grow to be more like Him.

Jesus is our ultimate role model. He has given us a pattern to follow and sent the Holy Spirit who will mould us into His image. If we follow in His footsteps we will be on the path to maturity.

Removing the rubble

Instead of the usual harsh shrill of my alarm clock, I was woken by the cheerful sound of birds singing and the welcome sensation of sun pouring in through the cracks of the curtains. I had taken the day off work and the weather was perfect! As I munched through my breakfast I made some plans to get my garden into shape. I would start at the far end, get to the middle by lunchtime, and finish by the evening. I strode out to the garden and looked over the first area I was going to work on, deciding to begin by digging it up. I picked up the garden fork, lifted it in the air and plunged it into the ground, expecting to hear the sound of earth retreating under the force of metal, but instead I heard a thud. I realised there must have been a stone under it and moved a little further along, but the same thing happened. I tried again and again in different patches of earth, but the result was always the same because someone had buried a pile of rubble there, and if there were any hope of growing flowers or vegetables, it would have to be cleared.

If we are to grow as Christians we must remove the rubble that is hidden under the surface of our lives. This may sound quite daunting but the Bible gives us some very practical guidelines, and in this chapter we will be concentrating on some which are given in Colossians.

Inside story

Jesus had some strong things to say about the religious leaders of His day. He described them as 'hypocrites' (Luke 11:44), and compared them to dishes that were clean on the outside but filthy inside, 'first cleanse the inside of the cup,' He challenged them, 'that the outside may be clean also,' (Matthew 23: 26). It is easy for us to condemn those men, but we have to be careful that the same thing cannot be said about us. That is why we are told make a determined effort to deal with sins which lie under the surface of our lives, which are exposed in these verses:

If then you were raised with Christ, seek those things which are above, where Christ is, sitting at the right hand of God. Set your mind on things above, not on things on the earth. For you died, and your life is hidden with Christ in God. When Christ who is our life appears, then you also will appear with Him in glory. Therefore put to death your members which are on the earth: fornication, uncleanness, passion, evil desire, and covetousness, which is idolatry. Because of these things the wrath of God is coming upon the sons of disobedience, (Colossians 3:1-5).

Sexual sins

We live in a society which has abused God's precious gift of sex, and become obsessed with it. Sex is used to sell products, increase the circulation of newspapers, and attract bigger audiences to films and shows. This makes it all the more important to tackle the sexual sins covered by the word 'fornication.' Today, sex outside marriage is considered to be normal, and it is even beginning to be accepted in some so called 'Christian' circles. I read an article in a newspaper about a lady, who was considered to be a Christian. The writer said that she, like many 'Christian' women of her generation practiced 'serial monogamy.' In other words, although she was not promiscuous, it was her practice to sleep with her current boyfriend. As far as the Bible is concerned, this is a sin which should have no place in a Christian's life.

When Christian young people are going out together they sometimes ask 'how far should we go?' The very fact they ask that question often indicates that they are heading for trouble. 'Fornication' includes all forms of sexual sin; you can get sexually intimate with someone without sleeping with them. Instead of asking 'how far we can go' it would be better to ask 'how pure can we be?'

Unclean thoughts

It was a huge Christian event, and a well-known speaker had been asked to speak at a late night youth meeting on sex and relationships. 'What do you think your most powerful sexual organ is?' He asked. There was a stunned silence; they wondered what was going to come next! The speaker waited a moment, and then answered his own question by saying it was the mind. If we are going to deal with sexual sins we will need to go back to the unclean thoughts they begin with, and this is what Paul is describing when he speaks of 'uncleanness.' Although this would include the act of 'fornication', the word probes deeper to uncover the thoughts and motives, which lead to it. Imagine you come into your kitchen to find the floor soaked because a tap had been left running. You can mop the floor to clear up the immediate mess, but if you do not get to the source and switch the tap off, your kitchen will soon be flooded again. If we are going to deal with sexual sins, we must get to the source, and deal with the thoughts and intentions leading to them, so that we may lead pure lives.

We should begin by setting our sights in the right direction. If we are caught up with the things of this world we are going to be polluted by its values. Paul, however, tells us to 'set (our) minds on things above, not on things on the earth' (Colossians 3:2), which will fill us with a desire to please Christ, not ourselves.

Many Christians spend time praying to know God's will for their lives, and although the Bible does not tell us where we should work, who we should marry, or which Church to belong to, it gives very specific guidance about our lifestyle. 'It is God's will that you should be sanctified: that you should avoid sexual immorality; that each of you should learn to control his own body in a way that is holy and honourable,' (1 Thessalonians 4: 3-4 NIV). Since God has made His will in this area so clear, we should be praying for purity each day. If we do this, we will be much more sensitive to the things which threaten to pollute our minds and affect our actions.

In cities you will see many cyclists wearing facemasks to filter out fumes which would harm them; we have to filter out the harmful influences around us. Do not sit in front of the television uncritically taking everything in; think about the underlying message and compare it to what God's Word has to say. Find out what a programme is like before you watch it, so that you can decide whether it is wholesome or not. Pastor and author Kent Hughes says: 'it is impossible for you to maintain a pure mind if you are a television watching "couch potato." In one week you will watch more murders, adulteries, and perversions than our grandfathers read about in their entire lives.'[10] It is much better to deal with these things in their early stages before they get a grip on us. Use the criteria that is given in Philippians 4:8: 'whatever things are true, whatever things are noble, whatever things are just, whatever things are pure, whatever things are lovely, whatever things are of good report, if there is any virtue and if there is anything praiseworthy—meditate on these things.' If a television programme, a newspaper story, or a joke does not fit this—do not bother with it!

Lusts

You have arrived home, stumbling under the weight of the box you have just carried from the car. You cannot wait to get it open because it contains your new, state-of-the-art computer. The next few hours are spent poring over instructions, unraveling wires, and plugging them in. Finally, everything is in place and you are ready to switch your machine on. The light blinks, there is a burst of noise as the fan comes on, and your screen springs into life, but progress suddenly come to a halt with the message 'install drivers.' It will not take you long to learn that your computer will not function properly if drivers are not installed. And if you want to stop something working you can do so by disabling its driver.

Thoughts, intentions and desires drive us; some are good and some are bad, but in Colossians 3 Paul is thinking about the things we must disable; 'passion' which is a drive that will not rest until it is satisfied, and 'evil desire'. When we are determined to please ourselves, no matter what God's Word says, we are being driven by 'passion' and 'evil desires'. This will lead us further from God and deeper into sin; we have to take action!

Nowadays, there is a lot of emphasis on 'preventative medicine', it is better to deal with a condition in its early stages, or even take steps to stop it coming about, than to treat it when it is more advanced. Similarly, we should do something about these drives before we find ourselves in a situation where we are faced with temptation. There are three steps we must take.

Firstly, we should consciously set out to please God, not ourselves. When we are tempted to give in to one of these desires, our aim to please God will lift us to a higher set of values and override our feelings.

Secondly, we should live in the power God has given us to overcome these things. I used to live near a museum that housed an old 'beam engine'. Once a week it would be started up, and it was a very impressive sight! There was a lot of power generated, but it did not actually do anything other than moving the two beams of wood. This is similar to the understanding of power many Christians have; it is something to experience, enjoy, and enthuse about—but it does not lead to anything practical, which could not be further from the truth! Peter tells us that God's 'divine power has given to us all things that pertain to life and godliness' (2 Peter 1:3). God gives us power as we step out in obedience to His Word. Think of a young child learning to walk. The parent holds her arms and guides her, but the child will be using her own muscles as she moves in the direction she is being led. This is how God's power works in our life; it is given to us as we put His Word into practice and go in the direction He has told us to. It is no good walking into an 'adult' shop and asking God to give you the power to resist temptation, you should be asking God to help you look the other way and walk past it!

Thirdly, we should put an alternative in its place. Later on in Colossians 3 Paul tells us to 'put off the old man' (verse 8), and 'put on the new man' (verse 10). Christian Counsellor, Jay Adams, speaks of this as 'dehabitutation and rehabituation.'[11] He says that when we 'turn our back on old ways' we 'must turn to face God in new ones.'[12] One way I encourage married men to do this, is when they are tempted to look lustfully at another woman, to pray for their wives. This not only steers them away from danger; it develops a very positive practice and provides an effective tactic to resist the pull of sin. It is 'dehabituation and rehabituation.'

Greed

In the film 'Wall Street' a wealthy businessman, sums up the spirit of the age by saying 'greed is good.' People are never satisfied with what they have; they must accumulate more wealth, increase their possessions and improve their standard of living. The Bible calls this 'covetousness' (Colossians 3:5) which is an insatiable drive to accumulate more.

This is normal in our society. You only have to turn on the television, open a newspaper, or walk past a billboard to be told that you need to buy a better car, take an exotic holiday, or own a more powerful computer. And it does not matter if you do not have the money to pay for it—you just enter into a credit agreement and get yourself into debt! Of course, there is nothing wrong with having these things. The problems begin when we pursue them and put them at the centre of our lives. That is why Paul goes on to call this idolatry; our desire to increase possessions and expand wealth can become so important that it occupies the place in our lives we once gave to God. If you want to check that you are not greedy, think about a possession, which is important to you, and ask yourself what your reaction would be if it were to be taken away from you. If you think you would be devastated you're in trouble!

How do we go about removing this particular piece of 'rubble'? The answer is given to us in Romans 12.

'I beseech you therefore, brethren, by the mercies of God, that you present your bodies a living sacrifice, holy, acceptable to God, which is your reasonable service. And do not be conformed to this world, but be transformed by the renewing of your mind, that you may prove what is that good and acceptable and perfect will of God.' (Romans 12:1-2).

We begin by taking a step back, looking at our whole life, and committing every part of it to God, so that we are living sacrifices 'holy, acceptable' to Him. In the Old Testament, animals were offered as sacrifices to God. In addition people were to bring a more personal sacrifice—obedience! David spoke about this when he said: 'Sacrifice and offering You did not desire; My ears You have opened. Burnt offering and sin offering You did not require. Then I said, "Behold, I come; In the scroll of the book it is written of me. I delight to do Your will, O my God, And Your law is within my heart' (Psalm 40:6-8). And when Samuel rebuked Saul for offering sacrifices without authorisation from a Priest, he said 'Has the Lord as great delight in burnt offerings and sacrifices, as in obeying the voice of the Lord? Behold, to obey is better than sacrifice, And to heed than the fat of rams' (1 Samuel 15:22). We no longer need to offer sacrifices because Jesus has fulfilled them, but our lives must be completely committed to Him, so that they are 'living sacrifices.'

Then we must make a conscious break with the world. J.B Phillips gets the point across very powerfully in his translation of these verses when he says 'do not let the world around you squeeze you into its own mould, but let God re-mould your minds from within.[13]' This is another instance where we need to 'filter out' influences around us. The next time you see an advert telling you how much you need a certain car, or to go on an expensive holiday, remember Jesus' words: 'Take heed and beware of covetousness, for one's life does not consist in the abundance of the things he possesses' (Luke 12:15).

Although we must do everything possible to avoid greed, we need not go to the opposite extreme and renounce every possession. James tells us that 'every good gift and every perfect gift is from above, and comes down from the Father of lights' (James 1:17). If you can afford a brand new car or to live in a big house, thank God for the way in which he has blessed you. Just remember to keep your eye on the giver rather than the gift!

Spiritual growth is upward and inward. We grow up into Christ's likeness as our lives are cleansed from the sinful habits cluttering them. It is not an easy process, but God has given us every resource we need. He will give us the power, but we must put in the work and remove the rubble.

Stumbling blocks or stepping stones?

The house was quiet, every member of my family was fast asleep, and the world outside was still plunged in darkness, but for an 'early bird' like me it was a great opportunity to catch up on some writing. I crept out of bed, made myself a cup of tea, sat down at my desk, and switched on my computer. There was no 'writers block' that morning, my fingers danced around the keyboard as they tried to keep up with the words pouring from my mind. By the time the family had woken up, I had finished a chapter and felt as if I was well on the way to completing the whole book. A few hours later I backed up my work onto a compact disk, and left the study; 'if I go on at this rate,' I thought, 'I'll have the book finished by next week.' I should have known better!

After breakfast I strode up the stairs, burst into my study, and sat down at my desk, raring to go, but my computer was in a very different mood. Every time I tried to get it to do something it stubbornly refused, until I had to resort to telephoning the technical help line. The person on the other end of the telephone told me to do all sorts of things, press all manner of keys, and click the mouse on countless items, but nothing seemed to work. Eventually he spoke words that strike terror into the heart of every computer owner—'how do you feel about re-formatting your hard disk?' This would solve the problem but I would lose everything held on my computer, and use up a lot of time re-installing the software. However, there seemed no alternative, so I agreed, re-assuring myself that I had saved everything important—including the work I had done earlier that morning, onto a compact disc. Several frustrating hours later the computer was working again. I got out the disc on which I had saved my morning's work and began to transfer it onto my computer—and everything stopped working again. As soon as I took the disc out everything was satisfactory. The problem all along was the disc on which I had saved my work, so not only had I wasted a morning following the instructions given by the help line, I had lost my work!

When I sat down to write this chapter I wanted to explain how we should see set-backs, difficulties, and trials as opportunities to grow, rather than obstacles to be cleared as quickly as possible. Not just the 'big league' like serious illness or bereavement, but the minor players too—a project that goes horribly wrong, a car that does not start, a baby who sleeps through the day and cries all night, or a colleague who makes life difficult. When these kind of things come our way we can either stumble over them or use them as stepping stones for growth. James says 'count it all joy when you fall into various trials, knowing that the testing of your faith produces patience. But let patience have its perfect work that you may be complete, lacking nothing' (James 1:3-4). His letter was one of the earliest in the New Testament, so you would assume that the trials he speaks of would be the big problems faced by the early Christians, such as persecution or martyrdom. But he uses a word which includes every difficulty you could mention. Big or small, major or minor they matter to God and if we have the right approach, they will help us to grow.

At first this does not look like an easy or rational approach. How could I 'count it all joy' when a mornings' work had been vandalised by my computer? What is the point in gritting your teeth and saying 'praise the Lord', when your holiday gets cancelled, your neighbour builds an extension that cuts out your light, or your central heating goes wrong? But James does not want us to wear a false smile and pretend everything is fine when it is not. Imagine you are calculating how you are going to pay your bills for the month; you find there is a shortfall, but you know that in a few days time there will be some money coming to you. You would count it into your calculation, and that is the idea James has. He uses a word which was used in accounting, we should 'count' every difficulty we face as a source of joy, because God will use it to make us 'mature and complete' (James 1:4 NIV). There is one quality we will need -'patience.' Instead of complaining, panicking, or trying to find the quickest way out, we should look to God, and trust Him to use it for His purposes and our maturity. R.T. Kendal describes this as 'dignifying trials', saying 'counting it all joy is to dignify God's providence because it shows that you can see God's hand in every area of your life.' Let us look at how we can use some of the most common things that happen to us as stepping-stones to growth.

Personal attacks

He had been stoned, shipwrecked, whipped, attacked by mobs, and thrown into prison; but the hardest trial of all was when people whom he had led to Christ, and taught, and encouraged, turned against him. Paul had spent eighteen months establishing a Church in Greece but after he left they were visited by some people exuding excitement, offering new experiences, and with teaching that appeared to be more sophisticated than his. The closer they got to these new teachers, the more they looked down on Paul; they decided his teaching was simplistic and his preaching weak. 'He is powerful in his letters, but very unimpressive in person' they said (see 2 Corinthians 10:10). This must have been like a knife in Paul's heart, he would have been hurt and disappointed—but he used it as a stepping stone!

Paul was never a man who stood on his own authority and demand respect. Although there were times when he reminded people that he was an apostle and defended the integrity of his ministry, he always responded to personal attacks with humility. When the Corinthian Christians called him weak and ineffective he spoke of God's strength which was perfected in his weakness, saying 'when I am weak, then I am strong' (2 Corinthians 12:10). Humility is a key factor for spiritual growth, John MacArthur says it 'creates the vacuum that divine grace fills. It is the benchmark of any useful servant of God'[14], and a personal attack provides an opportunity to exercise it. The next time it happens to you, do not rush to defend yourself, 'humble yourself under the mighty hand of God' (1 Peter 5:6) and leave your defense with Him.

When we come under this kind of attack we can easily become negative towards the people involved. Paul, however, took a very different approach; 'If I love you more,' he said to the Corinthians, 'then will you love me less?' (2 Corinthians 12:15 NIV). It is easy to love people who are kind to us, but Jesus said this is not enough. He said: 'love your enemies, bless those who curse, and do good to those who hate you, and pray for those who spitefully use you and persecute you' (Matthew 5:44). Paul put this into practice; 'when we are cursed, we bless; when we are persecuted, we endure it; when we are slandered, we answer kindly' (1 Corinthians 4:12 NIV). As we go through similar experiences we should show the same kind of love; and remember, it is not an impossible task because this is one of the fruits of the Spirit (see Galatians 5:22).

Uncertainties about the future

He lived in a palace, he had servants at his beck and call and a huge army at his command; but David's future suddenly looked very uncertain. He compared himself to a dead man who had been forgotten, and a broken vessel (Psalm 31:12). He said he heard slander all around him, and spoke of a conspiracy to assassinate him (Psalm 31:13). Yet, as David poured his troubles out to God, his trust grew stronger. He spoke of God as a fortress he had taken refuge in (Psalm 31:2), He asked Him to snatch him from the trap his enemies had set for him (Psalm 31:4), and he said 'my times are in your hands' (Psalm 31:15).

We would all prefer our circumstances to be stable, but uncertainty can break into life without warning. Redundancy can loom, health can break down, and these things will test our trust in God. When this happens we have a great opportunity to see ourselves as we really are and learn to depend on Him. The principle is a very simple one; Jesus told us to remember that our heavenly Father cares for us, and to stop thinking about tomorrow, take each day at a time, and concern ourselves with His Kingdom (see Matthew 6: 25-33).

Unwanted relocations

It is Monday morning. You force yourself to get out of bed, have your quiet time, rush through your breakfast and set out for work. Although you've had a great weekend you do not mind that it's Monday because you enjoy your job and feel very settled in your office. You have not been at your desk long when the boss asks to speak to you. He asks you about your weekend, congratulates you on the way you have been working, talks about a future project and then he drops his bombshell: 'I'd like you to move to our Birmingham office to work on this project.' For a moment you are speechless; you are flattered that he considers you competent enough for the task, but horrified at the prospect of an upheaval, and you are aware that, although this is given to you as a request, you do not have much choice in the matter!

Few people relish the thought of an upheaval, but it is reassuring to remember that God is sovereign and 'works all things according to the counsel of His will' (Ephesians 1:11). A great evangelist was stopped in his tracks by a prison sentence. His 'crime' was preaching the Gospel, and his future became uncertain; it was even possible that he could lose his life. Some people who he had led to Christ heard about this and became very troubled by the news. The evangelist sent them a letter, saying that his difficulties hadn't stopped his work, they had extended it! He had been spreading the good news in prison, and had been able to reach people who had been inaccessible to him until now. 'I want you to know, brethren, that the things which happened to me have actually turned out for the furtherance of the gospel, so that it has become evident to the whole palace guard, and to all the rest, that my chains are in Christ,' (Philippians 1:12-13).

The evangelist was Paul and his arrest and trial had become a talking point in the city he was imprisoned in, so the local Christians were using this as an opportunity to tell others about Jesus. He says that: 'most of the brethren in the Lord, having become confident by my chains, are much more bold to speak the word without fear,' (Philippians 1:1).

GK Chesterton said 'an inconvenience is an adventure wrongly considered and an adventure is an inconvenience rightly considered.' Relocations are God's tool to shake us out of complacency, teach us to trust Him more, and provide us with new opportunities. Life has a way of throwing up some unwelcome surprises, but if we want to grow in our Christian lives it is essential we see these things as stepping stones rather than stumbling blocks.

Building on failure

There can be few things as dispiriting as a sense of failure, especially when you feel that you have let the Lord down. Such 'failures' come in all shapes and sizes. You have been handed a golden opportunity to tell someone about Jesus but have passed it by. The difficult person you work with has caught you on a bad day, pushed you too far, and had a taste of your temper. An old habit, which you thought you had conquered, creeps back into your life. You make a terrible mistake and the fall-out is massive. Your Christian life loses momentum and your commitment to God's work grinds to a halt.

When things like this happen to us, the last thing on our mind is spiritual growth, but with the right approach we can build on them, get our lives back on track, and carry on growing. We are going to spend the remainder of this chapter thinking about how we can do so.

Answering the accuser

When you fail, do you tell yourself that you have let the Lord down so badly there is no hope for you? If so you cannot have been hearing from God, because the Bible speaks of 'godly sorrow' which 'leads to repentance and salvation' (2 Corinthians 7:9). Although we will find this painful, it is never destructive; it will lead us to seek forgiveness, effect a change and restore our relationship with God. Satan, however, wants to pull us down and persuade us to give up the Christian life; he is 'the accuser of the brethren' (Revelation 12:10), and we should be aware of his tactics. He destroys, but God builds!

James says 'submit to God. Resist the devil and he will flee from you,' (James 4:7). When we feel as if we have failed, we need to ask the Lord to show us where we have sinned, seek His forgiveness, ignore the thoughts Satan puts into our mind, and get on with the Christian life. We can do this by filling our minds with some relevant verses from the Bible. Psalm 103 tells us that God 'has not dealt with us according to our sins, nor punished us according to our iniquities,' (Psalm 103:10). And John promises that 'if we confess our sins, He is faithful and just to forgive us our sins and to cleanse us from all unrighteousness,' (1 John 1:9).

Learning from mistakes

I once had a guitar teacher who was very quick to spot a mistake. Playing a piece of music she would go back to the places where I had gone wrong, find out the cause, and help me to overcome it. We need to treat our mistakes in the same way. Instead of wasting time regretting them, we should give the matter prayer and thought. We do so by asking God to search our hearts and show us how we went wrong, and think of what it tells us about ourselves. Then we should see what the Word of God has to say about the matter, establish steps to make sure it does not happen again, and pray about them each day, for a period of time.

A Famous 'failure'

He exuded bravery and defiance in the face of death and danger: 'I'm not going to let them kill you Lord,' he said, 'they'll have to get past me first!' But on the same night Peter denied that he knew Jesus. Three days later Jesus rose from the dead, met with Peter and assured him that he still had an important role in the work which lay ahead, and on the day of Pentecost he preached to a crowd of thousands.

If you think you have failed, compare yourself to Peter and take encouragement from the way in which Jesus forgave him, re-instated him, and went on to use him so powerfully. Failure can be painful, because it shows us things about ourselves we would rather not know. But we can use these things to identify our weaknesses, bring about change, and grow.

The power of biblical thinking

It was the philosopher Descartes who said 'I think, therefore I am,' and there can be no doubting that thoughts affect actions. We have all met negative thinkers who cannot see the positive side of anything. As a result they are miserable, pessimistic and defeatist. On the other hand there are people who have a completely different attitude. They take problems in their stride, seize any opportunity that comes their way and make the most of their circumstances. There is nothing particularly new about this, in fact the Old Testament tells us that as a man 'thinks in his heart, so he is' (Proverbs 23:7). Our thoughts have a direct bearing on our actions.

When we first came to Christ we were given a new nature (2 Corinthians 5:17) which has affected every area of our lives, especially our thoughts and attitudes. As we grow in Christ we will become more disciplined and mature in the way we think. In this chapter we are going to look at the important role of our thoughts and attitudes in spiritual growth.

The Bible and the brain

An American Pastor, called Dr. Rufus M. Jones, often spoke about the importance of the mind, and when he preached he would try to get people thinking about the Bible. One day he received a letter from a member of his Church who did not agree with him. 'Whenever I go to church,' he said, 'I feel like unscrewing my head and placing it under the seat, because in a religious meeting I never have any use for anything above my collar button!'[15] I do not know what Dr. Jones wrote in his reply, but I do know that nothing could be further from the truth! The Bible places great emphasis on the way we think.

In the Old Testament there are a number of words that relate to the mind. The 'heart' often speaks of the mind as the centre of thinking and reason. But it also describes the will, the emotions, and the 'inner person.' It is the place where the word of God is received and it determines our words and actions. Proverbs often speaks of the heart in this way. We are told to incline our ear to wisdom, and apply our heart to understanding (Proverbs 2:2). And 'when wisdom enters' the heart, discretion preserves us, and understanding keeps us (Proverbs 2:10). The commandments are to be bound continually upon the heart, and written on 'the tablets' of our hearts (Proverbs 6:21; 7:3).

The Old Testament regards the mind as more than the location of our mental faculties. It is linked with a word that translates 'spirit', 'wind', or 'breathe.' The basic idea of the word is 'air in motion' which carries the image of life and vitality, and it also describes 'the entire immaterial consciousness of man.'[16] That is why David says: 'Blessed is the man…. in whose spirit there is no deceit. (Psalm 32:2) and Solomon is able to tell us that 'he who is slow to anger is better than the mighty, and he who rules his spirit than he who takes a city' (Proverbs 16:32).

'Soul' is another word relating to the mind. The Hebrew word can mean 'life', but its emphasis is usually on the individual. That is why we read of a soul being 'greatly troubled' (Psalm 6:3). When David says that he lifts up his soul to God he gives us a vivid picture of his dependence upon the Lord. And when he declares that his soul shall be joyful in the Lord he is talking about an individual and personal joy of which God is its source and focus.

The emphasis in the New Testament is on the change in our thinking which takes place after we are born again. We 'should no longer walk as the rest of the Gentiles walk, in the futility of their mind,' (Ephesians 4:17). Rather, we must be renewed in the spirit of our minds,' (Ephesians 4:23), and 'be transformed by the renewing of our minds' (Romans 12:2).

Out with the old—in with the new!

I will never forget the first Christian Camp I went to. My parents had taken me to Church since I was a child, but there did not seem to be any joy in the services. I could not understand why people bothered going! I had never been to the kind of meetings held at the camp before. People were enjoying themselves, they meant what they were singing, and they talked a lot about a 'new life' God had given them. Each evening one of the leaders directed the singing; he was so energetic it was a wonder he kept going! I can still picture him singing one of his favorite songs, his face beaming, his voice booming, and his arms outstretched to conduct us, as we sang 'what a wonderful change in my life has been brought, since Jesus came into my heart.' In the course of that week, what impressed me the most was the way in which he, and the other leaders, were living proof of the fact that Christ had changed their lives. I learned that being a Christian was not about believing a set of facts, but about being forgiven from sin, and receiving a new nature. Our new nature does not just affect the things we do, it also changes the way we think, and it is our responsibility to bring our minds into line with this. How do we do so?

We begin by setting our mind on the right course. The Old Testament promises that God will keep us in perfect peace when our mind is fixed on Him (Isaiah 26:3). And in Hebrews we are encouraged to fix our thoughts on Jesus (Hebrews 3:1 NIV) who is described as 'the apostle and High Priest' of our faith. Many of the problems we have with our thought life come because we are too occupied with ourselves and do not spend enough time thinking about Christ. There was a very moving story in my local paper. A lady was suffering from a deteriorating condition which left her unable to lift her head. This made life very difficult for her; even ordinary chores like going shopping and making a cup of tea were major challenges. Doctors warned her that if something were not done she would only have a few more years to live. Thankfully, she was successfully operated on and she celebrated by going to see a West End show, enjoying the luxury of being able to look up at the stage! Her experience illustrates the lives of many Christians. They are so absorbed with their own needs and burdened down with their own problems they have stopped looking up to 'where Christ is sitting, at the right hand of God' (Colossians 3:1), and as a result the Christian life has become a burden. Drawing on his wealth of pastoral experience, Martin Lloyd Jones said 'the people who give me the impression of being most miserable in their spiritual life are those who are always thinking of themselves and their blessings, their moods and states and conditions. The way to be blessed is to look to God; and the more we worship Him the more we shall enjoy His blessings.'[17]

If we are going to focus our minds on God we will need to be fixing them on heaven. To do this we must take our minds away from the things of this world, and set them 'on things which are above where Christ is, sitting at the right hand of God.' The Apostle Paul knew some people who had ignored this command and kept their minds on earthly things, and the result was disastrous. In fact Paul describes them as people 'whose end is destruction, whose god is their belly, and whose glory is in their shame—who set their mind on earthly things' (Philippians 3:19). Do not think you are immune from this danger! Spend a moment tracking the thoughts that have been occupying your mind today. What have they centred on—earthly or heavenly things?

One day I was listening to a Pastor who was about to retire, preach on Psalm 90. When he got to the verse which says 'teach us to number our days, that we may gain a heart of wisdom' (Psalm 90:12), he reflected on his decades in ministry. 'I wish I could have it all over again,' he said, 'it has gone so quickly.' At that point I had just marked ten years in the Ministry, and I was struck with the brevity of life and the time I had wasted dwelling on idle and anxious thoughts. The earthly things that occupy our minds so much of the time will pass, but the heavenly things will remain. Why do we spend so much time thinking about the former and so little time thinking about the latter?

Our new mind-set will change the way in which we think about circumstances which used to worry us. Every day brings a situation that has the potential to make us anxious, but we have been given a new nature, which will enable us to approach such things in a radically different way. Jesus told us not to have an 'anxious mind' (Luke 12:29). It is totally unnecessary because our heavenly Father cares for our every need. Jesus challenges us to think about this.

'Consider the ravens, for they neither sow nor reap, which have neither storehouse nor barn; and God feeds them. Of how much more value are you than the birds? "And which of you by worrying can add one cubit to his stature? If you then are not able to do the least, why are you anxious for the rest? Consider the lilies, how they grow: they neither toil nor spin; and yet I say to you, even Solomon in all his glory was not arrayed like one of these. If then God so clothes the grass, which today is in the field and tomorrow is thrown into the oven, how much more will He clothe you, O you of little faith?' (Luke 12:24-28).

Have you noticed the way in which Jesus repeats the word 'consider'? In the language this was originally written the word means to 'perceive clearly', or to 'understand fully'. It is used to describe Peter's full consideration of a vision (Acts 11:6). And it can be in found in Hebrews where we are called to 'consider one another in order to stir up love and good works' (Hebrews 10:24). In the verses we just looked at, Jesus uses the word to command us to resist anxiety by steering our thoughts in the right direction. He tells us to look at the way in which God cares for His creation and once we have done so we should draw a carefully considered conclusion. If God feeds the birds and clothes the grass He'll care for His children!

The new mind set will also affect our attitude towards other Christians. If you meet someone who seems to spend all their time criticizing the Pastor, Elders, Deacons and members of their Church, you can be sure their thinking is not in line with God's Word. This happened in the Church at Corinth, and Paul pleads with them to be 'perfectly united in mind and thought,' (1 Corinthians 1:10 NIV). The attitude we should adopt is nothing less than 'the mind of Christ' (Philippians 2:5). This will affect the way we relate to other Christians, we will 'consider one another in order to stir up love and good works' (Hebrews 10:24), and not swap insults or spread gossip. Take a minute to look at how you have invested your mental energy. Have you spent time carefully, and prayerfully, thinking about how you could be an encouragement to other Christians, or have you dwelt on the negative things. Be careful, the encouragers grow, but the discouragers crow!

Our approach to God's Word will be affected by the new mindset. When we read the Bible, with the help of the Holy Spirit, we use our minds to work through the implications and challenges in the passages of scripture that we read. This is what Paul is talking about when he tells Timothy to think about what he has been saying, promising that when he does so, the Lord will give him insight (2 Timothy 2:7).

It will spur us on to discipline our minds. We still have a sinful nature, and we will be affected by old thought patterns, but we are promised victory. However, God will not do what we can do, and His word calls us to 'gird up the loins of our minds' (1 Peter 1:13). This presents a picture of a person living in the first century gathering up his robes when he needed to move in a hurry. Peter uses it to tell us that we must keep a careful control of our thoughts, especially those that stray in the wrong direction.

A constant clean up operation

There are many grimy old buildings in London, but when one of them has been cleaned it stands out from the rest. The problem is not the stone with which it was constructed, but the dirt and fumes circulating in the air. Although the building stands out from the others, unless it is kept clean it will not be long before the dirt starts to settle again. Like that building, we are in danger of accumulating ideas and influences from the environment we live in, and it can happen without us noticing. The main sources of this are things we listen to, the conversations we have, and the television programes we watch. One day I called in to to see some Christians who were avid fans of a particular soap opera. I was greeted with a brief 'hello', ushered into the living room while they watched the end of the programme. On the screen, a man and a woman were sitting down to breakfast—they were not married and it was obvious they had slept together. Looking excited, one of the people I had gone to see turned and exclaimed: 'they've just spent the night together!' I do not think it had occurred to her that she had been watching something that glorified sin. And it made me consider the way many Christians suspend their thinking and accept these kind of values week after week, without pausing for thought, or comparing what they have seen with what God has said in His Word. If we listen to music, watch films, read books, or hear what people have to say without filtering these things through the Word of God, our thinking will soon be at the same level of the world around us. It is time to fight back! And that is what we will be thinking about in the next chapter.

Chapter 11

The battle for the brain

T he sun is shining, the sky is clear, and an excited group of spectators have taken their seats for the men's final at the Wimbledon Tennis Tournament. The players purposefully stride on to the court, exchange the customary warm up shots and begin their match. In the opening minutes one player excels. His serves are powerful and his returns keep his opponent running around the court. The crowd is captivated, and the commentators are excited, 'if he keeps this up he'll win in straight sets' they say. He wins the first set, falters in the second, fails to win it, and goes on to lose the match. After he walks off the court, shrouded in disappointment, he has to face a press conference. 'Why did you start so well and end so poorly?' He is asked. The player looks drawn and deflated, he shrugs his shoulders, takes a sharp intake of breath and says 'I just could not sustain it.' The commentators spend some time talking about the match, and one of them, a retired Champion says, 'you've just got to keep getting those shots back, or you lose'.

Ideas and images bombard us all the time. They must all be filtered and some of them should be rejected, but like that tennis player, we can have mixed success. Sometimes we find we are able to knock out an impure and ungodly thought that comes into our minds. But, other times we let it lodge and affect the way in which we think and act. We'll be thinking about how to keep on 'knocking them back in this chapter.'

Challenge your assumptions

The year was 1945, the Second World War was over and two excited girls were travelling home from the town they had been evacuated to. As a parting gift they were given a fruit which had not been available during the war – a banana. When midday approached the girls decided to have their lunch, they could not wait to taste this exotic new fruit they had been given, so they ate it first. They followed their instructions, peeled the skin and took their first bite; as soon as they did so the carriage was plunged into darkness. The girls were very young, they did not understand that the train was going through a tunnel. All they could think about was the fact that it was dark the moment they started to each the banana, and light when they stopped. When they reached their destination their mother was waiting to meet them. They told her all about the 'strange fruit', they had been given to eat, 'it makes everything go dark until you take it out of your mouth,' they said.

Like those little girls, we can make wrong assumptions, which affect the way we think and act. For example, a Bible Class teacher complains that he is not appreciated by his class, grows disillusioned and eventually gives up. His problem is not his unappreciative class, but the assumption that he needs to be appreciated. The Apostle Paul was one of the greatest teachers the Church has ever had, but he was seldom appreciated and often insulted. When he wrote to the Corinthian Christians he said: 'I care very little if I am judged by you or by any human court; indeed, I do not even judge myself. My conscience is clear, but that does not make me innocent. It is the Lord who judges me.' (1 Corinthians 4:3-4NIV). If the Bible class teacher compared his assumption with Paul's and discarded the desire for appreciation in place of approval from the Lord, he would never become so dispirited.

Assumptions shape our attitude and direct our actions, which is why we have to challenge them. Susan has been a Christian for three years; she is very involved in her youth group, and committed to the Lord. She has always been very popular, and has a large group of friends at college. They know she is involved in her Church, and they realise that her values are very different to theirs, but they have never heard her talk about her faith. This is a big problem for Susan, she knows what to say, and she has even worked out how to say it, but each time an opportunity arises, she worries what her friends will think about her and keeps silent. What is at the root of her problem? Susan would probably say it was fear, or nervousness; but her real obstacle is a wrong assumption, which has created a pattern of behaviour. Above all, Susan wants to be popular, and she assumes this will change when she tells her friends about her faith. If she is going to overcome this difficulty, Susan must change the assumption that it is important to be popular. This should not be too difficult, as Jesus has said 'woe to you when all men speak well of you', (Luke 6:26). Once she has thought and prayed about this she will be ready to speak up and talk about her faith when she has opportunity. But if she does not, this pattern will continue.

The Bible tells us to examine ourselves (1 Corinthians 11:28; 2 Corinthians 13:5, Galatians 6:4) and, since our assumptions have such an important effect on us, we should spend time prayerfully considering them. We can start by making a note of some of the things we have regretted doing over the past few days, and asking ourselves why we did them. Then we can dig a little deeper to uncover the assumption behind it. You may have been rude to someone close to you by telling them to stop nagging when they asked you to do something. Ask yourself why you perceived it in this way, and whether you might have misunderstood them, then think about it from their point of view. The next step would be to consider it in the light of God's Word. Is the problem the 'nagging' you thought you had been subjected to, or your own impatience? Galatians cites patience as 'fruit of the Spirit' (Galatians 5:22), so your impatience cannot be defended! It was not caused by another person's actions but by your old nature. Having faced up to the real cause of your reaction, you can take on a new assumption. The next time you are asked to do the same thing, it can be an opportunity to exercise the patience God gives when we 'walk in the Spirit' (Galatians 5:22).

We all remember how difficult learning to drive was, and the frustration of making the same mistake time and time again. A good teacher will help you overcome this by watching carefully, looking for the reason you are making the mistake, and helping you to correct it. Mistakes and failures can be very discouraging, especially when they are things we have done before. But rather than sink into a mood of despair we should trace the thinking that lay behind it and change the way we think.

Direct your thoughts

Whether we have an IQ of five hundred or five, our minds are always active. It is no good to allow our thoughts to wander in any direction, we must take control of them, and that will involve us taking some practical steps.

First, we must choose what we are going to think about. We have already looked at the way in which Paul encourages us to do so in Philippians: 'Whatever things are true, whatever things are noble, whatever things are just, whatever things are pure, whatever things are lovely, whatever things are of good report, if there is any virtue and if there is anything praiseworthy—meditate on these things.' (Philippians 4:8). If we are to make a conscious effort to fill our minds with the things listed here, our thoughts will begin to change. Sadly, many Christians choose to dwell on negative things, re-live bitter experiences, and rehearse arguments; it is no wonder that their spiritual growth is stunted!

A young man had a great future ahead of him. His wealthy father showered him with gifts and promised him security and stability. More significantly God had shown him that, in the future, he would be in a position of great authority. His brothers reacted to this news very badly. They were jealous of his close relationship with their father. Their envy grew to hatred, which became so intense that they talked about killing him. One of the brothers disagreed and persuaded them to sell him to some slave traders. Decades later their land was ravaged by famine. Desperate for food, they travelled to Egypt and pleaded with a high-ranking official for grain. The official they met was their brother, Joseph, and they were terrified that he might take revenge on them. 'Do not get agitated, or get angry with yourselves,' he told them, 'God has sent me ahead of you to save lives' (Genesis 45:5). How was Joseph able to be so positive? He chose to keep his mind off the pain and humiliation he had suffered at his brothers' hands and on God's purposes. That is why he was able to say 'you meant evil against me; but God meant it for good' (Genesis 50:20).

Secondly, we can select some positive things to think about. The best thing we can fill our minds with is the Word of God. If you do not have a good memory, write a verse down on a piece of paper, look at it throughout the day and spend some time thinking about it. Important as the Bible is, we do not have to be thinking about it every moment of the day. There are many other wholesome things we could think about. A sport, a family occasion, a hobby, or a holiday we might be planning. However, we should never forget that these things are gifts from God, otherwise we may put them before Him. A. W. Tozer said 'those who have been spiritually enabled to love God for Himself will find a thousand fountains springing up from the rainbow-circled throne and bringing countless treasures which are to be received with reverent thanksgiving as being the overflow of God's love for his children.'[18]

Thirdly, we must have a positive strategy for dealing with unhelpful thoughts. If we are going to put these things out of our mind we need something else to put in their place. An effective way of doing this is to pray for someone in need—there is something very powerful about putting someone else at the centre of our thoughts and then turning them to God. Paul spent much time in prison, but he rarely thought about himself, he was too busy praying for other people. He told the Christians in Ephesus that every time he prayed he could not stop giving thanks for them, and asked God to give them 'a spirit of wisdom and revelation in the knowledge of Him' (Ephesians 1:16). You only have to glance through his prayer at the beginning of his letter to see that he spent time focusing on their need and praying for their growth. No wonder he was able to say that he had learned to be content in all kinds of circumstances! (Philippians 4:11).

That is our battle plan! And if we follow it we will experience the benefits of disciplining our minds. But it is not going to be easy, and we need to be sure to sustain our efforts.

Growing with the family

When the great Evangelist, John Wesley, was going through a difficult time, he sat by the fireplace wondering why his spiritual life had become so dry and listless. While he was deep in thought he picked out a coal left by the side of the fire, and watched as its glow disappeared and it returned to its normal colour. Suddenly he realised how similar this was to his own experience; being busy with the demands of his work, he had neglected the Church, become isolated, and lost his fire. He needed to spend time with other Christians!

Although spiritual growth is personal, it is not individual; God has brought us into a community of people who encourage one another to grow. The writer to the Hebrews tells us to 'consider how we may spur one another on towards love and good deeds' and warns us 'not give up meeting together, as some are in the habit of doing', but to 'encourage one another—and all the more as you see the Day approaching,' (Hebrews10:24-25 NIV). The message is clear—if we want to grow we need to be part of a Church.

What is the Church?

To many people who are not Christians the word 'church' is associated with a building used for weddings, funerals, and services, but the definition given by the Bible is quite different. The Greek word for 'church' means 'a called out assembly', describing a community of people gathered by God. There is a **universal church**, which stretches across time consisting of every believer who has ever lived. Membership, of this 'called out assembly' though, can only come through new birth. And there is a **local church**—a group of Christians meeting in a particular place. This is the seed-bed in which God puts us to grow in our Christian life, reach the world around us, and help other Christians to grow.

A portfolio of pictures

In the New Testament there are several pictures of the Church, illustrating different aspects of its life and character.

It is God's family; we share a common bond with our heavenly Father but, as with human families, we cannot choose our relatives, so there will be some people we do not find particularly easy to get on with. Paul uses this image of the Church to urge us to work hard at our relationships, saying 'let us not become weary in doing good, for at the proper time we will reap a harvest if we do not give up. Therefore, as we have opportunity, let us do good to all people, especially to those who belong to the family of believers,' (Galatians 6:9-10 NIV). Do not be surprised when you discover tension in your Church; see it as an opportunity to put God's grace into action. The Bible gives us very clear instruction on how we are to do so.

I, therefore, the prisoner of the Lord, beseech you to walk worthy of the calling with which you were called, with all lowliness and gentleness, with longsuffering, bearing with one another in love, endeavoring to keep the unity of the Spirit in the bond of peace,' (Ephesians 4:1-3).

When the Church is pictured as a bride, we have a beautiful insight into our union with Christ. Paul compares a husband's care of his wife to Christ's care of His Church.

'Husbands, love your wives, just as Christ also loved the church and gave Himself for her, that He might sanctify and cleanse her with the washing of water by the word, that He might present her to Himself a glorious church, not having spot or wrinkle or any such thing, but that she should be holy and without blemish. So husbands ought to love their own wives as their own bodies; he who loves his wife loves himself. For no one ever hated his own flesh, but nourishes and cherishes it, just as the Lord does the church. For we are members of His body, of His flesh and of His bones. "For this reason a man shall leave his father and mother and be joined to his wife, and the two shall become one flesh." This is a great mystery, but I speak concerning Christ and the church,' (Ephesians 5:25-32).

In the Old Testament God compared the way his people were worshipping idols, to a bride deserting her husband (Hosea 1:2), and spoke of a day when He would be united with His people again (Hosea 2:17-20). Christ fulfills this in His relationship with the Church, and this will be complete when he gathers us at His return (see Revelation 19:7-9).

There are several instances in which the Church is pictured as a building. Paul makes use of it in 1 Corinthians to explain the way in which God used different people to help them at each stage of their development. When he led them to Christ, he was 'the master builder' who 'laid the foundation', and other men built on it (1 Corinthians 3:10); but God was the owner and designer. In 1 Timothy the church is pictured as 'the house of God … the pillar and ground of the truth,' (1 Timothy 3:15), this reminds us that the Church must be built on the Word of God. Peter uses the picture of a building to focus on worship, describing members of Christ's Church as 'living stones' who 'are being built into a spiritual house, a holy priesthood, to offer up spiritual sacrifices acceptable to God through Jesus Christ,' (1 Peter 2:5).

The Church is also a body. It consists of people who have been given different gifts and functions. Paul says 'there are diversities of gifts, but the same Spirit. There are differences of ministries, but the same Lord. And there are diversities of activities, but it is the same God who works all in all,' (1 Corinthians 12:4-7). And in Romans we are told that 'as we have many members in one body, but all the members do not have the same function, so we, being many, are one body in Christ, and individually members of one another,' (Romans 12:4-5).

A place to belong

Everyone wants a place where they belong; we have one—it is the local Church. This is where we will be taught from God's Word, cared for by other Christians, and helped by our Pastor and Elders who have a responsibility for our spiritual welfare. The first local Church met in Jerusalem. Most of its members had become Christians on the day of Pentecost, they met regularly continuing 'steadfastly in the apostles' doctrine and fellowship, in the breaking of bread, and in prayers,' (Acts 2:42).

We must not forget our responsibility to those who lead us. Hebrews tells us we must 'obey' the leaders of our local Church and 'submit to their authority' because 'they keep watch over us as men who must give an account,' (Hebrews 13:17 NIV). If these verses were taken more seriously, a huge burden would be lifted from the shoulders of many Pastors and

Elders, and the churches they lead would be able to make a lot more progress. Sadly, complaints and rebellion waste time and prevent Churches from growing. We must be sure to avoid getting caught up in this; otherwise our own development will be affected.

We do not have a passive role in the local church; God has given each of us a gift. It may be a more visible work like teaching, leading and evangelism; or it may be something like administration, encouragement, and hospitality, which keeps us in the background. Whatever it is, we have a responsibility to put it to use in our local church.

How do we find out what our gift is? Instead of sitting back and waiting for a sign to drop from heaven, we should look out for needs, pray and think about whether we can help, and, if we can—get on and meet them. This may not have a hundred percent success rate—there will be instances where we discover that we do not have the qualities we thought we had. But we can only find out by trying, and God will honour our willingness to serve, and lead us into other areas of service. Another thing we can do is to speak to our Pastor and Elders. They are responsible for 'the equipping of the saints for the work of ministry' (Ephesians 4:12), and will be able to identify our gifts and put them to use.

Growing through giving

It is sad to hear so many people complaining that they do not get anything out of the worship, sermons or house groups at their Church. This is not the attitude the Bible tells us to have; our aim should be to give rather than take; the more we give to God and to others the more our Heavenly Father will give to us. Jesus said 'give and it will be given to you: good measure, pressed down, shaken together, and running over will be put into your bosom. For with the same measure that you use, it will be measured back to you' (Luke 6:38). Spend some time before your worship service, or your house group, thinking and praying about how you can give to God, encourage others and help to build up the Church.

We cannot grow in isolation—God has made us part of His Church. He has given us gifts which complement each other, work towards a common goal, and enable us to develop in our individual relationship with God and our corporate life as God's family.

Growth targets

He sat in a prison cell, a soldier standing either side of him. Any day he would hear the result of his appeal to the Emperor. What was it going to be—life or death, a few more years to serve the Lord or the sharp end of the executioner's sword? Surprisingly, this was not at the forefront of Paul's mind; he was more concerned about the young believers he had led to Christ. He wanted them to grow in their faith, get through their difficulties and tell others about Jesus.

Hundreds of miles away these people met together as a church to pray for Paul and to think about what they could do to help him. Many of them had fond memories of his first visit to their city. Lydia, a local businesswoman, remembered her first encounter with Paul. Philippi was such a pagan city that they could not even muster up the ten men required for a synagogue to be opened, so each Saturday they met by the river to pray. Lydia first met Paul at one of these meetings; she realised that he had a message from God and she was eager to listen to him. As soon as he told her about Jesus she responded and became a Christian.

As plans were discussed, the local jailer's mind went back to his first encounter with Paul, which became a turning point in his life. He first met him in the prison, and it did not take him long to realise that Paul was different to the usual prisoners put in his care. He was not agitated or aggressive, as many others were; he seemed content, in fact he and his friend Silas were singing songs about Jesus into the night! The jailer could vividly remember the sensation of the earthquake that hit Phillipi on the night Paul was in prison and the terror which engulfed him. It was such a huge quake that the prison doors flew open and he assumed the prisoners had escaped. His blood ran cold; he was going to pay for this with his life— he might as well end it now. So he took out his sword, lifted it in front of him and braced himself for the cold steel which would be piercing him at any moment. Suddenly he became aware of a prisoner shouting out to him. 'Stop, you mustn't harm yourself, we are all here!' It was Paul, the man who had already made such an impression on him. The jailer led him out of his cell door to talk to him, and asked what he needed to do to be saved. Paul told him to 'believe on the Lord Jesus Christ', and from that day, both he and his family lived for Jesus.

As he tried to imagine Paul in his prison cell he could not help smiling to himself. He was certain that Paul would be making the best of his experience—by now every prisoner and guard would have heard the good news about Jesus!

Paul was very special to these people; he had told them about Jesus, helped them take their first frail steps in the Christian life, and got their Church on its feet. They had to do something to help him, so they decided to send Epaphroditus, one of their leaders, to give Paul a gift and tell him how concerned they were about him.

Epaphroditus' journey was long and hard. At one stage he had been so ill that he almost died. Eventually he arrived at Paul's prison cell and told him everything that had been going on in the Church. There were a lot of positive things, but some gave cause for concern. Two of the women were at loggerheads, and everyone in the Church knew about it. Some people were unsettled about Paul's imprisonment and anxious about what would happen to them if he were to be executed. Paul listened to Epaphroditus tell him about these things, but he did not seem to be worried by them. Their growth did not depend on his efforts but on God's power. He was confident that God would complete the work He had begun (Philippians 1:6).

At the end of Epaphroditus' stay, Paul handed him a letter to be read out to the Church. Lydia, the jailer, and the other Christians had been at the heart of his prayers. He had been praying for their spiritual growth, and he began the letter by telling them precisely what he had been praying for. This prayer can be found at the beginning of Paul's letter to the Philippians, and it provides us with some very clear targets for growth.

I thank my God upon every remembrance of you, always in every prayer of mine making request for you all with joy, for your fellowship in the gospel from the first day until now, being confident of this very thing, that He who has begun a good work in you will complete it until the day of Jesus Christ; just as it is right for me to think this of you all, because I have you in my heart, inasmuch as both in my chains and in the defense and confirmation of the gospel, you all are partakers with me of grace. For God is my witness, how greatly I long for you all with the affection of Jesus Christ. And this I pray, that your love may abound still more and more in knowledge and all discernment, that you may approve the things that are excellent, that you may be sincere and without offense till the day of Christ, 11 being filled with the fruits of righteousness which are by Jesus Christ, to the glory and praise of God. (Philippians 1:3-10).

Two ingredients

Although he was confident that God was going to finish His work in them, Paul had been praying for them to do their part by supplying two essential ingredients for growth. First, stretching the Greek language as far as it could possibly go he said he had been praying for their love to 'abound more and more in knowledge and depth of insight' (Philippians 1:9). This would be knowledge of God, which comes from the things He has revealed about Himself in the Word, and a personal relationship with Him. They were to put this knowledge into practice through 'depth of insight.' Which is a quality that would enable them to make a right decision when faced with moral dilemmas. They were going to need this as they lived for Christ in their pagan culture.

Secondly, Paul had also been praying that they 'may be able to approve the things that are excellent' (Philippians 1:10). 'Approve' was a word used to describe the way in which coins were tested to see whether they were authentic. And 'what is best' spoke of something superior. If they were going to grow they must invest their energies and resources carefully. This was going to require a re-evaluation of their priorities and some radical changes in their lifestyle.

Three goals

As well as praying for these essential ingredients for growth, Paul had been asking God to help them set some goals.

First, they must aim to be sincere (Philippians 1:10). He chose a word which had the same kind of meaning as holding something up to the light to see if it is genuine. It was often used in the market place. There would have been some shoddy traders in Philippi, who disguised cracks in pottery by filling them with wax and glazing them over. Any pottery they bought would be scrutinized by holding it up to the light. Paul had been asking God that they would make sure their lives could bear scrutiny from a watching world. There should be no 'cracks', or inconsistencies, which come to light when they are looked at a little more closely.

Secondly, they must aim to be 'without offence' (Philippians 1:10) This word depicts a person who is careful not to stumble or to put obstacles in anyone else's way. There is always a danger of having an attitude or acting in a way, which sets a poor example to new Christians and is a bad witness for the Gospel. This must be avoided at all costs.

Thirdly, they must aim to be 'filled with the fruits of righteousness' (Philippians 1:11). Their whole lives must be characterised by 'the conduct—the actions, words, and thoughts—that God Himself judges to be right.'[19] To aim for this they must put God at the centre of their lives and seek to please Him in everything they were to do. And by doing so they would accelerate their spiritual growth.

Five hundred miles had been crossed, and many weeks had passed before Epaproditus finally arrived back in Philippi to tell the excited Christians his news of Paul and read out the letter. The jailer smiled to himself again, he knew Paul would make the best of his situation! Lydia sat and nodded as she listened to these details of Paul's prayer, and everyone's heart was stirred. God was going to finish the work He had begun—but He had given them essential ingredients and important targets to help them do their part. They have been given to us too, let us be sure to make use of them and grow for God!

Notes

1 ibid
2 **Lucas, RC** , *The Message of Colossians and Philemon,* IVP Leicester 1980, page 39
3 **Piper, John,** *The Pleasures of God,* Christian Focus Publications 1998, page 137
4 **Bridges, Jerry,** *The Pursuit of Holiness,* Navpress 1996, page 17
5 **Green, Michael,** *2 Peter and Jude,* IVP Leicester 1968, page 151
6 **Stott, John,** *The Message of Ephesians,* IVP Leicester 1979, page 81
7 **Packer, JI** , *God's Words,* IVP Leicester 1981, page 159
8 **Grudem, Wayne,** *Systematic Theology,* Zondervan Publishing House, Grand Rapids, Michigan, page 831
9 See John 3
10 **Hughes, Kent,** *Disciplines of a Godly Man,* Crossway Books, Wheaton Illinois,1991, page 29
11 **Adams, Jay,** *The Christian Counselor's Manual,* Zondervan, Grand Rapids, Michigan, 1973, page 191
12 ibid. page 188
13 **Phillips, JB,** *The New Testament in Modern English,* Wyman and Sons Ltd. Reading, 1959, page 332
14 **MacArthur, John,** Humility: *The Benchmark of Useful Ministry,* 'The Master's Seminary Mantle' Winter 2000, Master's Seminary, Los Angeles
15 Quoted by John Stott in 'Your mind matters', IVP 1972, page25
16 **Harris, Archer, and Waltke,** *Theological Wordbook of the Old Testament,* Moody Press, Chicago 1980, vol2 page 837
17 **Lloyd Jones, Martyn,** *God's Ultimate Purpose,* Baker Book House, Grand Rapids, Michigan, 1994, page 58
18 **Tozer, AW** *Renewed Day by Day,* OM Publishing,
19 **Carson, DA,** *A Call to Spiritual Reformation,* IVP Nottingham1997, page 134

Study guide

CHAPTER 1: THE GROWTH GENE

1 Think about the way you have reacted to difficulties at home, work and in your church. What does this tell you about your level of spiritual maturity?

2 Read 2 Peter 3:17-18 and 1 Corinthians 3:1-3.
What effect does lack of spiritual growth have upon our relationship with Christ, and those in the local church?

3 Look up 2 Corinthians 10:15, 2 Peter 3:18, and Colossians 1:10, and identify three areas in which we are to grow. Think about the practical things which will enable us to do so.

4 Use Psalm 139:23-24 as a pattern for a time of prayer, asking the Lord to help you see areas of your life in which you need to grow.

CHAPTER 2: GOD-CENTRED GROWTH

1 Take a large sheet of paper and draw a line dividing it into two. On one side list the reasons why you want to grow. Then read Ephesians 1:6-14 and, on the other side, note down the reasons Paul gives. How do the lists compare and what do they tell you about your motivation to grow?

2 Read Philippians 1:6 and 2:12-13. What do these verses tell us about God's work in us? What is our responsibility?

3 Look at 1 Peter 2:2, Hebrews 5:11-14, and Ephesians 5:15-21. List the things we need to be doing if we are going to grow.

4 Write down the things you most want in life (and be honest).
Where does spiritual growth come into it? What does it tell you about your priorities? Spend some time in prayer, asking God to help you make any necessary changes in your life.

CHAPTER 3: GOD AT WORK!

❶ Read Matthew 5:48, Ephesians 4:13, and James 1:4. [Perfect speaks of wholeness or completeness].
What do these verses tell about the goal we should be working towards? How far do you think you have progressed?

❷ Look at 2 Peter 3:18, what are the two factors of spiritual growth given here?
How would you define them?
How can you grow in them?

❸ Read Colossians 1:10 and look back on the past week, asking yourself whether your actions, thoughts, and attitudes have been pleasing to God.

❹ List the negative qualities Paul speaks of in Ephesians 2:1-10. What does this tell us about our condition when God began His work in us?
Contrast it with the positive qualities in Ephesians 2:5-6.

CHAPTER 4: THE MASTER PLAN

❶ Look at 1 Thessalonians 1:4, Ephesians 1:4, and John 15:16. Did we choose God or did He choose us?

❷ What effect should this have on our attitude towards spiritual growth (see Colossians 3:12, 2 Peter 1:10)?

❸ What is the work God has done in us (John 3:3)?
How is it possible (1 Peter 2:24)?
How does He do it (Titus 3:5)?
What effect does it have on us (2 Corinthians 5:17)

❹ Read 1 Corinthians 15 and describe the last part of God's plan. How should this shape our attitude towards this life?

❺ How does spiritual growth fit into this master plan?

Study guide

CHAPTER 5: THE MASTER BUILDER

❶ Read Acts 20:23-38.
What dangers did Paul see facing the church in Ephesus?
Why was he confident they could face them?
What did they need to face such a challenge?

❷ Look at 1 Peter 1:23 and 1 Peter 2:2. What role does the Word of God play in our new birth and our spiritual growth?

❸ Think about how much the Word shapes your life. Are there any areas you have left untouched?

❹ If our Bibles were taken from us, how much of the Word would you be able to retain? Consider what this tells you about your knowledge of God's Word and how you can improve it.

❺ What is the most effective way of keeping God's Word in our mind (see James 1:22-25)?

CHAPTER 6: THE MASTER TOOL

❶ Read John 17:14-16. Jesus speaks of us being in the world but not of it. Think about the implications of this for your social life and work.

❷ Look at 1 Thessalonians 4:3 and John 17:17?
What is sanctification?
Why is it an important part of spiritual growth?

❸ Read 1 Thessalonians 5:24 and Philippians 2:12-13. What do these verses tell us about the balance between what God is doing in our lives and what we must do?

❹ When will we reach perfection (see Philippians 3:21)?
How should this encourage us when we find the Christian life difficult?

❺ Would someone who is not a Christian be able to say you are different? If the answer is no, what do you think you should be doing about it?

CHAPTER 7: THE PERFECT PATTERN

❶ Think about the people who have influenced you the most. Is the Lord Jesus the biggest influence on your life? If the answer is 'no', think about how He should become so.

❷ Read Luke 4:1-13
What does Jesus use to overcome temptation?
How does this help us?
Think about the way in which Satan twists the Bible in order to tempt Jesus. What does this tell us about the importance of handling God's Word correctly?
(see 2 Timothy 2:15)

❸ What does Mark 14:41-42 tell us about Jesus' submission to His Father? Compare this to Hebrews 12:2-3. Think about the things you least want to do or face. How does Jesus' example help you?

❹ Think of how you have reacted to an injustice in your life and compare it to Jesus' reaction in 1 Peter 5:21-22. Pray that your reactions would be more like Jesus'.

CHAPTER 8: REMOVING THE RUBBLE

❶ Write a list of television programmes you have watched and books and magazines you have been reading in the last month. Then read Philippians 4:8. How do they match up to the qualities listed there?

❷ Read 1 Thessalonians 4:3-4. Paul says this is God's will for us. How much of a priority has it been for you? What can you do to put it into practice?

❸ Colossians 3:8 tells us to 'put off the old man', while verse 10 says 'put on the new man.' What does this tell us about the positive and negative steps that we must take in order to deal with sin in our lives?

❹ Look at Colossians 3:1-5, asking God to show you which of the sins listed here have a hold on your life. Think about how you can 'put them to death', and set out some goals which will help you to do this.

Study guide

CHAPTER 9: STEPPING STONES?

❶ Look at James 1:3-4.
How do you 'count it all joy when you fall into various trials'? Compare this to your own attitude towards difficulties you have faced and write down what you will need to do to put this into practice.
What is the relationship between trials and spiritual growth?

❷ What guidance does 1 Peter 5:6 give you when you are under personal attack?

❸ What does Psalm 31 tell us about the way in which uncertainty can deepen our relationship with God?

❹ Read Philippians 1:12-13. How was Paul able to see his imprisonment as an opportunity rather than a problem?
Think about problems you face and look at ways in which they can be seen as opportunities. Spend some time praying about this.

CHAPTER 10: BIBLICAL THINKING

❶ List the things which have occupied your mind in the last couple of days. What proportion of time have you spent thinking about the things of this world?

❷ Read Matthew 6: 25-34.
What does Jesus say about worry?
What does our worry tell us about the extent to which we are trusting in God?
What is the key principle Jesus gives us to overcome worry?

❸ What does 1 Peter 1:13 tell us about the need to discipline our thought life?

❹ Look at Romans 12:1-2. What is the link between our thought life and our commitment to God?

CHAPTER 11: THE BATTLE FOR THE BRAIN

❶ Write down some of the things which you have most regretted doing recently and recall what led you to do them. Find out what the Bible says about them and consider how you can bring your thinking into line with God's Word.

❷ Read Genesis 37:1-28; 45:1-7 and 50:19-21.
Why was Joseph able to be so positive about the trauma he had been through? How does it compare to the way you think about difficult times?
What can you do in order to be more like Joseph?

❸ Using the principles set out in this chapter, put together a plan of action that will help you deal with unhelpful and ungodly thoughts.

❹ Memorise Psalm 19:14, and use it as a prayer each day.

CHAPTER 12: GROWING WITH THE FAMILY

❶ What comes into your mind when someone mentions 'church'?
How does it compare with the definition of 'a community of people gathered by God?'

❷ Look at Paul's description of the church in Acts 20:28. What are the implications for the way we should think about our local church?

❸ What does Acts 2:42 tell us about the early church's priorities?

❹ Pray about any problems in your church and ask God whether you are part of the answer or the problem.

❺ Read Hebrews 10:24-25 and think about ways in which you can encourage people in your church.

❻ Look at Romans 12:6-8 and ask God to help you to discern your gift and put it into practice in your local church.

Study guide

CHAPTER 13: GROWTH TARGETS

Read Philippians 1:3-10

❶   Spend some time meditating on verse 6, thanking God that He will complete the work He has begun in you.

❷   What is the link between love which 'abounds more and more', and 'knowledge' and 'discernment'? (verse 9) What do they tell us about our part in the work which God has begun in us?

❸   Why is it necessary to 'approve the things that are excellent' (verse 10)? How should this shape the way in which you invest your energy and resources? What corrections do you think you'll need to make?

Improving your
Quiet Time

Simon Robinson

144 pages   £6.95

Simon Robinson's *Improving your Quiet
Time* is full of practical advice which
should encourage many who are struggling
to achieve a better balance in their
Spiritual walk. It also contains ideas for
personal study plans, together with a two
year Bible reading plan.

REFERENCE: QT
ISBN 0 902548 89-1

A COMMENDATION FROM
JOHN MACARTHUR:

"This compact book gives
spiritual guidance on so
many areas of a Christian's
relationship with God.
A delightful, practical
how-to guide. Invaluable."

FROM EVANGELICALS NOW:

"Can be confidently
recommended as an
introduction to the
quiet time, and a stimulas
to those aiming higher
in their use of it"